The Art of Expression

by

William Walker Atkinson

Contents

CHAPTER I

EXPRESSION

IN THE volume of this series entitled "The Art of Logical Thinking," we have endeavored to point out to you the rules of logical mentation, and the methods best calculated to develop the faculty of logical thought. In another volume of the same series entitled "Thought-Culture," we have endeavored to instruct you in the principles and methods of developing the several faculties of the mind, so that you may use these faculties as efficient instruments of thought. The purpose of the present volume is that of pointing out to you the approved methods and principles of *expression*—the art of expressing the thoughts, ideas, desires and feelings within you.

The term "expression" is derived from the Latin word *expressus*, meaning "to squeeze out." And even in the present usage the idea of "squeezing out," or pressing out as the wine is pressed out from the grape, is present. "Expression" as used in this connection is defined as: "The act of expressing, uttering, declaring, declaration, utterance, representation; representation by words; style of language; the words or language in which a thought is expressed; phraseology, phrase, mode of speech; elocution, diction, or the particular manner or style of utterance appropriate to the subject and sentiment."

The Art of Expression is concerned chiefly with oral expression or speaking, but its rules and principles are equally applicable to expression by writing, or composition. As an authority says of one aspect of rhetoric: "It was originally the art of speaking effectively in public, but afterward the meaning was so extended as to comprehend the theory of eloquence, whether spoken or written. * * * Campbell considers the art the same as eloquence, and defines it as 'That art or talent by which the discourse is adapted to the end,' and states that the ends of speaking, or writing are reducible to four: to enlighten the understanding, to please the imagination, to move the passions, or to influence the will. Broadly speaking, its aim is to expound the rules governing speech or written composition, designed to influence the judgment or feelings. It includes, therefore, within its province, accuracy of expression, the structure of periods, and figures of speech."

For our purpose we may consider the Art of Expression as the art of efficient and effective communication between individuals by language. It is not a *science*, observing, uncovering, discovering, disclosing and classifying, but an *art* applying the results of prior scientific investigation and classification. As Hill well says: "Logic simply teaches the right use of the reason, and may be practiced by the solitary inhabitant of a desert island; but rhetoric (one aspect of the Art of Expression), being the art of *communication* by language, implies the presence, in fact or in imagination, of at least two persons—the speaker or the writer, and the person spoken to or written to. Aristotle makes the very essence of rhetoric to lie in the distinct recognition of a hearer. Hence its rules are not absolute, like those of logic, but relative to the character and circumstances of those addressed; for though truth is one, and correct reasoning must always be correct, the ways of communicating truth are many. Being the art of *communication by language*, rhetoric applies to any subject matter that can be treated in words, but has no subject matter peculiar to itself. It does not undertake to furnish a person with something to say; but it does undertake to tell him how best to say that with which he has provided himself."

Before one can successfully apply the Art of Expression, he must first have *something to express*. In order to express thoughts and ideas, one must first have evolved these thoughts and ideas. As Coleridge well says: "Style is the art of conveying the meaning appropriately and with perspicuity, whatever that meaning may be. But some meaning there must be, for in order to form a good style, the primary rule and condition is—*not to attempt to express ourselves in language before we thoroughly know our own meaning.*"

It is not our purpose to attempt to make orators or elocutionists of the readers of this book. The phase of expression which is manifested in public speaking is better taught by the many text books on oratory or elocution, although we shall have something to say regarding the arrangement and general expression of one's ideas that may be useful to the public speaker. Our purpose, however, is rather to impress upon the ordinary individual the methods and principles of correct, clear and forcible expression of his ideas in the ordinary walks of life. Whoever has communication with his fellowmen should learn to express his ideas and thoughts to them in a clear, correct and forcible manner. Not only the man selling goods to others, but also every one who has social or business dealings of any kind with others, should acquire the art whereby he may impress his ideas upon the others forcibly and clearly.

Correct *expression* results in clear *impression*; forcible *expression* results in distinct and deep *impression*. There is a corresponding *impression* resulting from every *expression*. Campbell's classification of the four ends of speaking or writing, *viz.* (1) To enlighten the understanding; (2) to please the imagination; (3) to move the passions; (4) to influence the will; describes the four classes of *expression*. The results arising from these expressions are always found to be *impressions*— the understanding, imagination, passions or will, respectively are *impressed* by the respective forms of *expression* appropriate to each.

Every person expresses himself in some way; often in a very poor way. To some the process of expression is easy and pleasant while for others the words will not flow, and the sentences fail to include the spirit and meaning of the thought or idea behind it. This does not always arise from the fact that the person has no clear ideas or thoughts; for, on the contrary, many very clear thinkers find themselves unable to transmute their ideas into words, and fail to express themselves with the clearness, force and effect to which their mental creations entitle them. There are but few people who do not feel hampered in the expression of their ideas and thoughts by the lack of understanding of the fundamental principles of the Art of Expression. These fundamental principles are simple, and the methods of applying them may be easily acquired.

But it is not our desire or purpose to consider Expression as an art separate and apart from the practical necessities of everyday life and business—as an art concerning itself with grace and beauty rather than with utility. This is a utilitarian age—the test of truth and merit is "what is it good for;" "how will it work;" "what can we do with it;" "what is its practical use?" And so, in our consideration of the Art of Expression we shall endeavor to remember, first, last and always the demand of the age—the what-can-we-do-with-it requisite. It is not enough that one should be able to clothe his thoughts in beautiful verbal garb. It is demanded that the clothing of words shall be adapted to well withstand the rough requirements of everyday wear, and of practical usage. Remembering always that expression precedes impression, and that impression is essential to the practical process of communication with others, we shall endeavor to show the forms and methods of expression best adapted to producing the strongest, clearest and most lasting impressions upon the minds of others.

The salesman who indulges in beautiful speech, but who fails to impress the prospective purchaser with the merits and desirability of his wares is not a successful salesman. The business correspondent, who is able to compose a letter which is a gem of literary style, but which, nevertheless, fails to convince the person addressed of the merit of the proposition discussed, is not a successful correspondent. The salesman is expected to "land the order;" the correspondent is expected to win over the persons to whom his letters are addressed; the advertising man is expected to attract the attention and awaken desire in the minds of those who see and read his advertisements; in fact, each and every person who has anything of importance to communicate hopes to convey his meaning to those with whom he communicates by word of speech or written lines. And so, while "style," in the sense of beauty and literary merit, has its place, still it is not the important requisite in the practical communication of the world of men and women of affairs of to-day.

In order to apply the Art of Expression to meet the requirements of practical modern life, not only must the form and construction of sentences be considered, but much attention must be paid to the psychology of words and phrases. Psychology has invaded the realm of rhetoric, and is rapidly asserting its right to an important place in the practical management of affairs. Rhetoric asks: "Is this beautiful; is it technically faultless?" Psychology asks: "Will this awaken the requisite understanding and thought in the minds of those for whom it is intended; will it attract the attention, hold the interest, arouse the desire, convince the understanding, and arouse the will of those to whom it is addressed?" Therefore, the Art of Expression is closely connected with The New Psychology, and appropriately is included in the series of books upon the general subject of the latter. This is the keynote of our conception of the subject which we shall consider in this book. We strive not to teach expression for the sake of expression, but rather *expression* as a method of *impression*. We consider the subject from the viewpoint of psychology, rather than from that of rhetoric. And we make this statement as an explanation—not as an apology.

serve as a form of language. Not only does man, or the animal, recognize these gestures by reason of having perceived them previously, and usually accompanied or followed by the appropriate and corresponding action, but they awaken in him an instinctive and involuntary imitative action or reaction which tends to produce in him an intimation of the mental feeling behind the physical movement or gesture. For not only does "thought take form in action," but "action induces feeling" in return, and an instinctive imitation of the outward physical movement arising from a feeling or thought tends to reproduce in the mind feelings or emotions corresponding to those which originally gave rise to the movement or gesture.

Bain says: "Most of our emotions are so closely connected with their expression that they hardly exist if the body remains passive." Maudsley says: "The specific muscular action is not merely an exponent of passion, but truly an essential part of it. If we try, while the features are fixed in the expression of one passion, to call up in the mind a different one, we shall find it impossible to do so." Halleck says: "By restraining the expression of an emotion we can frequently throttle it; by inducing the expression of an emotion we can often cause its allied emotion." James says: "Refuse to express an emotion and it dies. Count ten before venting your anger, and its occasion seems ridiculous. Whistling to keep up courage is no mere figure of speech. On the other hand, sit all day in a moping posture, sigh and reply to everything in a dismal voice, and your melancholy lingers."

Dr. Woods Hutchinson says: "To what extent muscular contractions condition emotions, as Prof. James has suggested, may be easily tested by a quaint and simple little experiment upon a group of the smallest voluntary muscles in the body, those that move the eye-ball. Choose some time when you are sitting quietly in your room, free from all disturbing thoughts and influences. Then stand up, and assuming an easy position, cast the eyes upward and hold them in that position for thirty seconds. Instantly and involuntarily you will be conscious of a tendency toward reverential, devotional, contemplative ideas and thoughts. Then turn the eyes sideways, glancing directly to the right or left, through half-closed lids. Within thirty seconds images of suspicion, of uneasiness, or of dislike, will rise unbidden in the mind. Turn the eyes on one side and slightly downward, and suggestions of jealousy or coquetry will be apt to spring unbidden. Direct your gaze downward toward the floor, and you are likely to go off into a fit of reverie or abstraction."

In view of the above facts of psychology, and considering that there is always present a tendency to instinctively imitate, at least faintly, the outward movement and gestures of others, we may see how there may be created or induced in the mind of the observer a sympathetic reproduction of the feelings or emotions experienced by the person giving the outward expression. We know how we are able to *interpret in feeling* the outward expression of an actor, or of a person in real life who is experiencing great joy or deep pain. There is a sympathetic state induced in us, by means of which we are able to interpret the feelings or emotions of others whose outward physical expression we may witness. In this way animals and savages are able to instinctively become aware of the feelings and thoughts of those with whom they come in contact. Their perceptive faculties being well trained and developed by use, and their emotional nature being usually unhampered, they have a "direct wire" of instinctive understanding open to them. We may thus understand the important part played by gesture in the early days of language.

It is astonishing how much may be conveyed by gesture, when the parties to a conversation fail to understand each other's language. There is a universal "sign language" which is understood by all races of men. The rubbing of the stomach and the pointing to the open mouth are the universal signs of hunger and demand for food. Resting the head on the hand and closing the eyes indicate the desire to sleep. Shivering indicates cold. The clenched fist shaken at another indicates defiance and the desire to fight. The uplifted open hands indicate nonresistance. The soft glance of the eye, and the encircling motion of the extended arms indicate love. And so on—these universal signs are understood by all peoples and races. A good pantomimist will be able to go through an entire play, without uttering a word, and yet clearly indicating each thought and feeling so that it becomes intelligible to the audience.

Quackenbos says of the use of pantomime among the ancient Greeks and Romans, with whom it was developed to a high degree, as indicating the power and force residing in this form of emotional expression and impression: "This fact was known and appreciated by the ancient Greeks and Romans, whose action was much more vehement than we are accustomed to see at the present day. On the stage, this was carried so far that two actors were at times brought on to play the same part; the office of one being to pronounce the words, and that of the other to accompany them with appropriate gestures, a single performer being unable to attend to both. Cicero informs us that it was a matter of dispute between the actor Roscius and himself whether the former could express a sentiment in a greater variety of ways by significant gestures, or the latter by the use of different phrases. He also tells us that this same Roscius had gained great love from every one by the mere movements of his person. During the reign of Augustus both tragedies and comedies were acted by pantomime alone. It was perfectly understood by the people, who wept and laughed, and were excited in every way as much as if words had been employed. It seems, indeed, to have worked upon their sympathies more powerfully than words; for it became necessary, at a subsequent period, to enact a law restraining members of the senate from studying the art of pantomime, a practice to which it seems they had resorted in order to give more effect to their speeches before that body."

The same authority continues: "When, however, the Roman Empire yielded to the arms of the Northern barbarians, and as a consequence, great numbers of the latter spread over it in every direction, their cold and phlegmatic manners wrought a material change as regards the gestures, no less than the tones and accents, of the people. The mode of expression gradually grew more subdued, and the accompanying action less violent, in proportion as the new influences prevailed. Conversation became more languid; and public speaking was no longer indebted for its effect to the art of the pantomimist. So great was the change in these respects that the allusions of classical authors to the oratory of their day were hardly intelligible. Notwithstanding these modifications, however, the people of Southern Europe, being warmer and more passionate by nature, are, at the present day, much more animated in their tones and more addicted to gesticulation than the inhabitants of the North. This is particularly true of the French and Italians."

CHAPTER III.

THE EVOLUTION OF LANGUAGE

FROM GESTURES and motions man evolved articulate speech, in its lower and higher degrees, and the basis of language was formed. But there must have been a period in which inarticulate sounds or cries formed the connecting link between gestures and speech. In fact, in all primitive languages we find these inarticulate cries and sounds reproduced in crude word-sounds. The sigh, the groan, the laugh, and the scream have their correspondences in the words of the lower races.

There have been many theories and hypotheses advanced to account for the origin of language, all of which are more or less plausible, but none of which seem to fully answer all the requirements. Until the nineteenth century it was the custom of writers to consider language as a direct revelation and gift from the divine being, but the trend of thought along the line of evolution has caused later writers to regard language as subject to the general evolutionary law, and to have gradually developed from the gestures and rude inarticulate cries of the higher animals and lower races of men.

Philologists seek to trace all languages from a few elemental root-words or sounds, but it must be remembered that even these sounds constituted an elementary language, and the beginning must be traced still further back. Monboddo, in his "Origin and Progress of Language," holds that man being but a higher species of ape began with an apelike language consisting of a few monosyllables, by which they expressed their feelings, desires and emotions. He holds that the sounds: *ha, he, hi, ho* and *hu*, variously grouped and accented formed the elementary language of the race. Murray, on the contrary, holds that all human language originated in nine monosyllables, namely: *ag, bag, dwag, gwag, lag, mag, nag, rag, swag*, each of which he says indicated a species of action. Of these monosyllables he says: "Power, motion, force, ideas united in every untutored mind, are implied in them all. They were uttered at first, and probably for several generations, in an insulated manner. The circumstances of the action were communicated by gestures and the variable tones of the voice; but the actions themselves were expressed in their suitable monosyllables."

Another authority says: "It is now generally conceived that the origin of language was contemporary with the origin or accentuation of gregarious instinct. There is supposed to have been a stage when the human species, living singly or in isolated families, began under the influence of natural exigencies to draw together in tribal companies. Among all gregarious animals we find more or less developed forms of signalling, as among herbivora. Possibly among some there is even complex communication, as the 'antennal language' of ants. The human species, subjected to the stress of social organization, similarly developed its first crude community of signs, which, in part because of man's superior powers of articulation, but mainly because of his intellectual supremacy, gave rise to organized speech."

While there is a general agreement among the authorities as to the necessities which gave rise to the birth and evolution of language, there is a wide range of opinion among them regarding the nature of the mental impulse which gave rise to the manifestation. One school holds to the idea that language arose from the "desire to communicate" felt by early man—the wish to communicate his thoughts and feelings to his fellows—which caused a spontaneous manifestation of elementary speech. Another school holds that the "desire to communicate" was a secondary and later development, and that speech originated in the natural expression of emotions, joys, feelings, pain, etc., uttered as a natural means of relief through expression which is still familiar to the race, but which was manifested without any desire or thought of communication. An authority says of this view: "It gained the character of language by reason of community of emotion. Thus, a certain cry became a word, either as instinctively interpreted by like-feeling and like-expressing fellows, or as the characteristic expression of a congregation of savages, brought together under social excitement; as, for example, a cry of dance or battle."

The later authorities hold that the last-mentioned view is the more scientific, and the trend of the latest thought on the subject seems to be in this direction. According to this view the *interjection*, as *ah! oh! hist! ouch!* etc., was the most primitive form of words used by man, and which arose naturally from emotional expression. As Quackenbos says: "The first words were, no doubt, interjections; for it would be natural for men, however savage or ignorant of the use of words, to employ exclamations for the purpose of expressing their sudden emotions. It is thought probable that these primitive interjections were given various and diversified shades of meaning by (1) syllabic variation; (2) by syllabic repetition; and (3) by a change or variation in pitch. Some have held that this third form of variation gave rise to a "sing-song" or chanting—a form of rhythmic speech, from which the later forms of language were evolved. It is POINTED OUT that even to-day the barbaric races indulge in war-chants, corn-chants, marriage-chants, etc., which consist merely of a rhythmic repetition of a few elemental interjections indicating feelings or emotions."

The authorities hold that many of the elementary words which succeeded this "sing-song" language were derived from the sounds arising from the natural objects expressed by the words, the impulse arising from imitation. In this way the natural cry, growl or other vocal sound of the animal would become its name. Instances of this may be observed among small children who apply to things the sounds emanating from them, as *"choo-choo"* for a locomotive; *"bow-wow"* for dog; *"moo"* for cow; *"bah"* for sheep, etc. It is a long stride, however, from these simple imitative words to general concepts. As an authority well says: "The stupendous step was the creation of conventionalized or symbolic expressions. An onomatopoetic utterance, as the bird's call meaning the bird uttering it, is directly incorporated in immediate experience; it is instinctive, as we observe with children. But when such utterances become universalized, meaning *all* birds or birds *in general*, whether gifted with like call or not, then we have the abstraction which lies at the base of all reasoning and makes intellectual evolution possible. Only the possession of a brain much superior to that of any other animal can have enabled man to develop a language adapted to reason from the primitive and instinctive signal language."

It is held that after the interjection, the *noun* was employed— for names were given to things, as above indicated. Then must have arisen the *adjective*, in order to distinguish between different things of the same kind by reason of their qualities; for instance, *"large* tree;" *"little* bush;" *"black* rock;" etc. From a similar need must have arisen the adjective pronouns *this* and *that*, and later the article *the*. *Verbs* must have sprung into use early in the history of language, as it is almost impossible to express a thought without the use of words indicating action. Following naturally upon the heels of the verbs must have come the *adverbs*.

Personal pronouns are held to have been among the later developments of language, as the need of them did not become evident until the intellectual processes of the race became more complex. Even to-day the savage races do not use the personal pronoun, but instead indicate the thing by its own name. Young children invariably repeat the noun instead of substituting the pronoun. The child says, "Give Jack Jack's top," instead of "Give me my top." "He, she and it" are foreign to its vocabulary. Quackenbos says of this: "So great, indeed, seems to be the disinclination of youthful minds to multiply terms that it is often found quite difficult to teach them the use of the pronoun. Such was the case, in all probability, with man in the infancy of his being; and it is not likely that he added this new species of words to his primitive and necessary stock until sufficient advance had been made in the formative process to show to their great advantage as regards brevity of expression and pleasantness of sound."

The last-mentioned authority also says: "Among the earlier races of men, it seems probable that there was much less said than at the present day. Their sentences were at once fewer, shorter, and simpler, than ours. As successive advances, however, were made, and it was found that mutual intercourse was a source of pleasure, men did not confine themselves simply to what it was necessary to communicate, but imparted freely to each other even such thoughts as had no practical bearing. The original brief mode of expression was gradually laid aside; longer sentences were used; and a new class of words was required to connect clauses so closely related in construction and sense as not to admit of separation into distinct periods. This was the origin of *conjunctions*; and the same cause, when man's taste was still further improved and he began to think of beautifying language while he extended his power of expression, led to the invention of the *relative pronoun*. * * * Man had now the means of expressing fully and intelligibly all that came into his mind; and his future efforts were to be directed, not to the creation of new elements, but to improving and modifying those already devised, to harmonizing the whole and uniting them in a consistent system. Up to this point necessity had operated; the improvements subsequently made must be attributed to the desire of pleasing."

Scaliger says: "Three things have contributed to enable man to perfect language,—necessity, practice, and the desire to please. Necessity produced a collection of words very imperfectly connected; practice, in multiplying them, gave them more expression; while it is to the desire of pleasing that we owe those agreeable turns, those happy collocations of words, which impart to phrases both elegance and grace."

CHAPTER IV.

WORDS

A WORD IS: "A single articulate sound, or a combination of articulate sounds or syllables uttered by the human voice, and by custom expressing an idea or ideas; a single component part of a language or of human speech."

Locke says: "Upon a nearer approach, I find that there is so close a connection between ideas and words; and our abstract ideas and general words have so constant a relation one to another, that it is impossible to speak clearly and distinctly of our knowledge, which all consists in propositions, without considering, first the nature, use, and signification of language."

Jevons says: "In endeavoring to reason correctly, there is nothing more necessary than to use words with care. The meaning of a word is that thing which we think about when we use the word, and what we intend other people to think about when they hear it pronounced, or see it written. We can hardly think at all without the proper words coming into the mind, and we can certainly not make known to other people our thoughts and arguments unless we use words."

Another authority says: "The speculation is sometimes advanced that if man were isolated he would lose the faculty of language. This is inferred from the premises that language is solely a means of communication of mind with mind. It is fair to affirm that psychology of recent years has established the fact that a large amount of our reasoning is mediated by language alone, and is made possible only through the abstractions which words enable. Since this is the case, man could not wholly lose the faculty of language so long as his mind remained rationally active. Need for the so-called 'internal speech,' the mental use of words, would persist, forming as it does one of the great utilities of language. * * * Thought is formulated in language, that is, is symbolized in words. These words, when uttered, are *understood*, as we say; that is, they are taken to be symbols of thought in another's mind. The thought of the person who utters the words, and the thought of the person who understands them, are supposed to be similar, although the thought of neither is to be identified with the symbolic conveyance—that is, with the language."

In a previous chapter we have seen that the involuntary gesture or instinctive sound expressing a feeling or emotion acts as the medium of communication between the person expressing it and other persons, by reason of the fact that there is an unconscious process of imitation of the sound or gesture in the mind of the other persons, and the consequent translation of this reproduced expression into real sympathetic feeling. Then again we see that the gesture or sound gradually becoming familiar is accepted as a *symbol* of the feeling or emotion—it becomes practically a *word*. Later on, names are applied to things and actions, and thereafter are accepted as symbols of the things they are intended to represent.

It will be found that the majority of the words understood by us are accepted merely as abstract symbols, without exciting any particular feeling or emotion. Others, which when first heard arouse feeling, gradually pass into the category of mere symbols on account of familiarity and repetition. Other words have a positive suggestive value, and induce a greater or lesser degree of sympathetic feeling by reason of their association, as for instance "mother," "home," "child," etc. An interjection expressing joy or pain tends to cause a sympathetic feeling in those hearing them. Other words, symbols of feeling or emotion, as for instance "love," "hate," "fright," etc., often tend to at least faintly awaken a sympathetic understanding in the minds of others. And words expressing sensations of taste, smell, touch, sight, or hearing, often have more or less actual suggestive force, and indicate a power to awaken a sympathetic response, as for instance: "sweet," "sour," "nauseating," "soft," "harsh," "stench," "shrill," "bright," "glaring," "red," "smooth," etc. The use of these suggestive and "sympathetic" words by speakers in descriptive speeches often proves very effective. This being realized, we may begin to understand the important part played by the right words in expressing one's ideas for the purpose of *impressing* others, and the necessity of the intelligent choice of words and the correct use thereof.

Jevons says: "There is no more common source of mistakes and bad reasoning than the confusion which arises between the different meanings of the same word. * * * In many cases the meanings of a word are so distinct that they cannot really lead us into more than a momentary misapprehension, or give rise to a pun. A 'rake' may be either a garden implement, or a fast young man; a 'sole' may be either a fish, or the sole of the foot; a 'bore' is either a tedious person, a hole in a cannon, or the sudden high wave which runs up some rivers when the tide begins to rise; diet is the name of what we eat daily, or of the Parliament which formerly met in Germany and Poland; ball is a round object, or a dance. In some cases a word is really a different word in each of two or three meanings, and comes from quite different words in other languages. * * * From such confusion of words, puns and humorous mistakes may arise, but hardly any important errors. * * * Any word which has two or more meanings, and is used in such a way that we are likely to confuse one meaning with another, is said to be ambiguous, or to have the quality of ambiguity. By far the greater number of words are *ambiguous*, and it is not easy to find many words which are quite free from ambiguity. Whether we are writing, or reading, or speaking, or merely thinking, we should always be trying to avoid confusion in the use of words but no one can hope to avoid making blunders and falling Into occasional fallacies."

In considering words in their relation to The Art of Expression we shall regard them from three viewpoints, viz., (1) The Supply of Words; (2) The Choice of Words; and (3) The Arrangement of Words.

It will be seen that before one is able to make a choice of words, or to arrange his chosen words in an effective manner, he must first have a number of words at his disposal. It follows that all else being equal, a person speaking or writing who has the largest vocabulary, or stock of words from which to choose, will be enabled to make a much better choice and a much more effective arrangement. One's vocabulary is his stock of the raw material of speech, from which he may weave or mould sentences which will serve to properly clothe the creations of his mind. And so, we shall first consider the Supply of Words, or the Building of a Vocabulary, from which we may select, choose and arrange our words with which we may desire to express our thoughts and ideas so as to impress them upon the understanding of others.

CHAPTER V.

Building a Vocabulary

A "VOCABULARY" IS: "The sum or stock of words used in a language; the range of words employed by an individual, or in a particular profession, trade or branch of science." Hill says: "Other things being equal, a speaker or writer who has the largest stock of words to choose from will choose the best words for his purpose. Hence the desirableness of an ample vocabulary."

There is a great range of difference in the vocabularies of different individuals. There is estimated to be one hundred thousand words in the English language. Marsh says: "There occur in Shakespeare's works not more than fifteen thousand words; in the poems of Milton not over eight thousand. The whole number of the Egyptian hieroglyphic symbols does not exceed eight hundred, and the entire Italian operatic vocabulary is said to be scarcely more extensive. Hill says: "The vocabulary of business has not been estimated, but it is certainly a small one. So is that which suffices for the ordinary necessities of a traveler. Poverty of language is the source of much slang, a favorite word, as *nice, nasty, beastly, jolly, awful, stunning, splendid, lovely, handsome, immense*, being employed for so many purposes as to serve no one purpose effectively. A copious vocabulary, on the other hand, supplies a fresh word for every fresh thought or fancy."

Herrick and Damon say: "For purposes of mere existence, a few hundred overworked words will answer well enough. It is safe to say, however, that such a small vocabulary implies a narrow range of thought. Words represent objects and ideas; generally speaking, a few ideas call for few words, and conversely, the use of few words indicates the possession of few ideas. As a rule, a man who has at the most a thousand terms for expressing his wants, his feelings, his reflections, has fewer wants, feelings, and reflections than the man who has two thousand words at his command. * * * To sum up, the chief reasons for cultivating a wide vocabulary are: first, because words, like pieces of money, represent wealth—the more symbols, the more ideas; second, because if we have three words or more that represent very nearly the same thought, we can distinguish just what we do mean more clearly (e. g., woman, lady, mother; house, residence, home; contrive, make, experiment, etc.); third, because variety rests the reader's mind and gives him enjoyment; fourth, because the possession of many words aids our exact understanding of writers who use many words to differentiate their ideas. Much valuable thought is misunderstood, or but half understood, when the reader has only a vague idea of the words used. In short, add to your store of words in order that you may have a richer mental life and that you may never be at a loss for the right word to use when you want it."

In order to build up a vocabulary it is necessary to become acquainted with the meaning of words; and in order to do the latter it is necessary to study words. Words may be studied in two ways: (1) by means of dictionaries and similar works; and (2) by means of the writings of the masters of literature, where the words may be studied in their context. Many great writers and speakers have deliberately studied the dictionary, learning to take a keen interest in words and their meanings. Rudyard

Kipling is said to find the keenest pleasure in the perusal of his favorite dictionary, and in detecting the subtle shades of difference between words of the same class. Lecky says that "Chatham told a friend that he had read over Bailey's English Dictionary twice from beginning to end." In studying words in the dictionary it is well not only to familiarize oneself with the looks and sound of the word and its exact meaning, but also to run down the word to its roots in order to obtain its real "essence." Many words have strange and unsuspected origins, and it is a fascinating task to dig into this mine and to uncover rich nuggets of this kind. Many, on the other hand, find that they obtain a clearer idea of the value, meaning and relation of words by carefully considering them in reading selections from good writers, and incidentally turning to the dictionary whenever an unusual or unfamiliar word is met with.

In connection with the study of words by means of reading the works of writers, Hill says: "Care should, however, be taken to educate the taste; for one who is familiar with the best authors will naturally use good language, as a child who hears in the family circle none but the best English talks well without knowing it. As, moreover, every person, however well brought up, comes in contact with those who have not had this advantage, hears from his companions or meets in the newspapers phrases such as he does not hear at home or meet in good authors, it behooves him to fix in his mind, as early as possible, the principles of choice in language."

The student of words—one who has learned to take an *interest* in words and their meanings—will find it advantageous to acquire the "note-book habit." By this is meant the habit of jotting down any unusual or unfamiliar word which one may hear in conversation, or meet with in reading; or some word which one hears used in an unfamiliar sense or form. Then, later in the day, when time permits, one may look up the words in the dictionary and add them to his vocabulary. If one thus notes only *one new word a day*, he will have added three hundred and sixty-five words in a year—no inconsiderable number, either, in view of the size of the average individual's vocabulary. If one will make a point of really *mastering* one word a day, he will find himself making rapid improvement in a few weeks. And the habit once acquired, new interest is created and "second-nature" results. In mastering the word not only should one familiarize himself with the looks of the word in print and in writing, but also with the actual sound of it when spoken by himself. He must not only *read* the word, but also *write* it and *speak* it. And, not only should he acquaint himself with the word itself, but he should also learn its synonyms, or words closely resembling it in meaning.

Synonyms may be learned from the dictionary, if the latter be good, but the student will find it useful to have at hand some good work on synonyms, of which there are a number, some of which may be obtained at quite a reasonable price. It is a good practice to search one's own memory for all the known synonyms which are related to the word being studied This being done, reference may then be made to the work on synonyms for further words to add to one's list. Another good practice is to write a sentence describing some thought in the mind of the student, and then to underline every word which one has repeated several times. Then endeavor to supply a proper synonym, so that, if possible, no verb or adjective shall be repeated in a paragraph or long sentence.

Fernald says: "Scarcely any two of such words, commonly known as synonyms, are identical at once in signification and in use. They have certain common ground within which they are interchangeable, but outside of that each has its own special province, within which any other word comes as an intruder. From these two qualities arises the great value of synonyms as contributing to the beauty and effectiveness of expression. As interchangeable, they make possible that freedom and variety by which the diction of an accomplished writer or speaker differs from the wooden uniformity of a legal document. As distinct and specific, they enable a master of style to choose in every instance the one term that is the most perfect mirror of his thought. To write or speak to the best purpose, one should know in the first place all the words from which he may choose, and then the exact reason why in any case any particular word should be chosen. To give knowledge in these two directions is the office of a book of synonyms."

To illustrate the above the following example from Fernald's "English Synonyms, Antonyms and Prepositions" will serve. Fernald gives the following synonyms for "*Conquer*:"

Beat	Overthrow	Checkmate	Prevail over
Crush	Put down	Defeat	Reduce
Discomfit	Rout	Down	Subdue
Humble	Subject	Master	Subjugate
Overcome	Surmount	Overmaster	Vanquish
Overmatch	Win	Overpower	Worst

A work like Roget's "Thesaurus" is useful in finding the word or words to fit an idea already formed in the mind. In a dictionary, one has a word and wishes to find its meaning; in the Thesaurus one has the meaning and wishes to find the word or words to fit it. Many persons who are well acquainted with the dictionary do not know that such a work as Roget's "Thesaurus" exists. It is a most valuable work for the student of words, and is sold at a reasonable price. We advise you to become acquainted with it.

Herrick says: "A wide vocabulary means freedom. We must become free of our language (as was said anciently of a town or state), if we are to express ourselves effectively and completely. Words are curiously human things; they carry with them romantic stories. Each one, no matter how unobtrusive it may seem, differs from its fellow, and is useful in its own way."

Palmer, in his "Self-Cultivation in English" says: "It is important, therefore, for anybody who would cultivate himself in English to make strenuous and systematic efforts to enlarge his vocabulary. * * * Let anyone who wants to see himself grow, resolve to adopt two new words each week. It will not be long before the endless and en· chanting variety of the world will begin to reflect itself in his speech, and in his mind as well. I know that when we use a word for the first time we are startled, as if a firecracker went off in our neighborhood. We look about hastily to see if anyone has noticed. But, finding that no one bas, we may be emboldened. A word used three times slips off the tongue with entire naturalness. Then it is ours forever, and with it some phase of life which had been lacking hitherto. For each word presents its own point of view, discloses a special aspect of things, reports some little importance not otherwise conveyed, and so contributes its small emancipation to our tied-up minds and tongues."

CHAPTER VI.

THE CHOICE OF WORDS

IN ORDER to speak or write clearly and forcibly it is necessary that we exercise an intelligent choice of the words in our vocabulary. As Hill says: "A writer or speaker should, in the first place, choose that word or phrase which will *clearly* convey his meaning to the reader or listener. It is not enough to use language that *may be* understood; he should use language that *must* be understood. He should remember that, so far as the attention is called to the medium of communication, so far is it withdrawn from the ideas communicated, and this even when the medium is free from flaws. How much more serious the evil when the medium obscures or distorts an object." And as Herrick says: "Even the newest of thoughts may be made to seem flat if tritely phrased; the most precise thinking looks vague if it is couched in generalities; the most dignified matter becomes trivial if it is overadorned. The demands upon our taste in the choice of words are manifold; every sentence is a new problem in diction."

The first essential in the choice of words is *clearness*. The faults opposed to Clearness are:

I. *Obscurity*, or the use and arrangement of words in such a manner that it is difficult to understand the real meaning thereof;

II. *Equivocation*, or the use and arrangement of words so as to render them capable of more than one interpretation;

III. *Ambiguity*, or the use and arrangement of words so as to leave the hearer in doubt between two opposing meanings or interpretations.

Macaulay was one of the clearest of writers. Morley says of him: "He never wrote an obscure sentence in his life." , Trevelyan says of him and his methods of work: "The main secret of Macaulay's success lay in this, that to extraordinary fluency and facility he united patient, minute, and persistent diligence. * * * If his method of composition ever comes into fashion, books probably will be better, and undoubtedly will be shorter. As soon as he had got into his head all the information relating to any particular episode in his 'History' (such, for instance, as Argyll's expedition to Scotland, or the attainder of Sir John Fenwick, or the calling in of the clipped coinage), he would sit down and write off the whole story at a headlong pace, sketching in the outlines under the genial and audacious impulse of a first conception, and securing in black and white each idea and epithet and turn of phrase, as it flowed straight from his busy brain to his rapid fingers. * * * As soon as Macaulay ·had finished his rough draft, he began to fill it in at the rate of six sides of foolscap every morning, written in so large a hand and with such a multitude of erasures, that the whole six pages were, on the average, compressed into two pages of print. This portion he called his 'task,' and he was never quite easy until he had completed it daily. More he seldom sought to accomplish; for he had learned by long experience that this was as much as he could do at his best; and except when at his best, he never would work at all. * * * Macaulay never allowed a sentence to pass muster until it was as good as he could make it. He thought little of recasting a chapter in order to obtain a more lucid arrangement, and nothing whatever of reconstructing a paragraph for the sake of one happy stroke of apt illustration. Whatever the worth of his labor, at any rate it was a labor of love."

The following paragraph from "Essay on Milton" will furnish a brief example of Macaulay's style:

"Ariosto tells a pretty story of a fairy, who, by some mysterious law of her nature, was condemned to appear at certain seasons in the form of a foul and poisonous snake. Those who Injured her during the period of her disguise were forever excluded from participation in the blessings which she bestowed. But to those who, in spite of her loathsome aspect, pitied and protected her, she afterwards revealed herself in the beautiful and celestial form which was natural to her, accompanied their steps, granted all their wishes, filled their houses with wealth, made them happy In love and victorious in war. Such a spirit is Liberty. At times she takes the form of a hateful reptile. She grovels, she hisses, she stings. But woe to those who in disgust shall venture to crush her! And happy are those who, having dared to receive her in her degraded and frightful shape, shall at length be rewarded by her in the time of her beauty and her glory!"

And yet as Hill says: "Clearness is a *relative* term. The same treatment cannot be given to every subject, nor to the same subject under different conditions. Words that are perfectly clear in a metaphysical treatise may be obscure in a didactic poem; those that are admirably adapted to a political pamphlet may be ambiguous in a sermon; a discourse written for an association of men of science will not answer for a lyceum lecture; *a speaker must be clearer than a writer*, since a speaker's meaning must be caught at once if at all."

Emerson says: "*Eloquence is the power to translate a truth into a language perfectly intelligible to the person to whom you speak.* He who would convince the worthy Mr. Dunderhead of any truth which Dunderhead does not see, must be a master of his art. Declamation is common; but such possession of thought as is here required, such practical chemistry as the conversion of a truth in Dunderhead's language, is one of the most beautiful and coherent weapons that is forged in the shop of the Divine Artificer."

Newman speaking upon the subject of the necessity of clearness in the use and arrangement of words says: "Reflect how many disputes you must have listened to which were interminable because neither party understood either his opponent or himself. Consider the fortunes of an argument in a debating society, and the need there so frequently is, not simply of some clear thinker to disentangle the perplexities of thought, but of capacity in the combatants to do justice to the clearest explanations which are set before them,—so much so, that the luminous arbitration only gives rise, perhaps, to more hopeless altercation. 'Is a constitutional government better for a population than an absolute rule!' What a number of points have to be clearly apprehended before we are in a position to say one word on such a question. What is meant by 'constitution!' by 'constitutional government!' by 'better!' by 'a population!' and by 'absolutism!' The ideas represented by these various words ought, I do not say, to be as perfectly defined and located in the minds of the speakers as objects of sight in a landscape, but to be sufficiently, even though incompletely, apprehended before they have a right to speak."

The best authorities give the following as *a general rule for clearness* in the use and arrangement of words: *Use particular terms in speaking or writing of particular objects; use general terms in speaking or writing of general objects.* Also, to secure clearness: *In the choice of words favor those which more nearly define themselves; and discard, those which are most capable of obscure, equivocal, or ambiguous interpretation.*

Pronouns are frequently the cause of obscurity, ambiguity or equivocation in interpretation of the sentences containing them. Clearness requires that a pronoun should refer, without question, to its one antecedent alone. Avoid ambiguous pronouns. The clearest and best writers never shrink from using a word twice, rather than to substitute a pronoun which fails to refer directly to its antecedent noun without a possibility of mistake. Freeman says of this: "I learned from Macaulay * * * never to be afraid of using the same word or name over again, if by that means anything could be added to clearness or force. Macaulay never goes on, like some writers, talking about 'the former' and 'the latter,' 'he, she, it, they,' through clause after clause, while his reader has to look back to see which of several persons it is that is so darkly referred to. No doubt a pronoun, like any other word, may often be repeated with advantage, if it is perfectly clear who is meant by the pronoun. And with Macaulay's pronouns, it is always perfectly clear who is meant by them." In the following paragraph from Macaulay, the pronoun "he" is used twelve times, and yet with perfect clearness and without ambiguity. This paragraph is a model, and is worthy of careful study and analysis:

> The situation of William was very different. He could not, like those who had ruled before him, pass an Act in the spring and violate it in the summer. He had, by assenting to the Bill of Rights, solemnly renounced the dispensing power; and he was restrained, by prudence as well as by conscience and honour, from breaking the compact under which he held his crown. A law might be personally offensive to him; it might appear to him to be pernicious to his people; but, as soon as he had passed it, it was, in his eyes, a sacred thing. He had therefore a motive, which preceding Kings had not, for pausing before he passed such a law. They gave their word readily, because they had no scruple about breaking it. He gave his word slowly, because he never failed to keep it.—MACAULAY: History of England.

The following quotations show the fault of the obscure or ambiguous pronoun:

"A tremendous fall of snow rendered his departure impossible for more than ten days When the *roads* began to become a little practicable, *they* successively received news of the retreat of the Chevalier Into Scotland."—SCOTT.

"*They* were persons of such moderate Intellects, even before *they* were impaired by their passion, that *their* irregularities could not furnish sufficient variety of folly."—STEELE.

"It was the loss of his son on whom he had looked with an affection *which* belonged to his character, with an exaggerated admiration *which* was a most pardonable exercise of his fancy *which* struck the fatal blow to his spirit as well as to his body."—MAURICE.

"Rasselas was the fourth son of the mighty emperor in *whose* dominions the Father of Waters begins his course; *whose* bounty pours down the streams of plenty, and scatters over half the world the harvests of Egypt."—JOHNSON.

Hill makes the following very proper criticism regarding the fault of "fine writing," which is also equally noticeable in the speech of many people who pride themselves upon the assortment of "choice terms:" "In *fine writing* every clapping of hands is an 'ovation,' every fortune 'colossal,' every marriage an 'alliance,' every crowd 'a sea of faces.' A hair-dresser becomes a 'tonsorial artist;' an apple-stand, a 'bureau of Pomona;' an old carpenter, 'a gentleman long identified with the building interest.' A man does not breakfast, but he 'discusses (or "partakes of") the morning repast;' he does not sit down at table, but he 'repairs to the festive board;' he does not go home, but he 'proceeds to his residence;' he does not go to bed, but he 'retires to his downy couch;' he sits, not for his portrait, but for his 'counterfeit presentment;' he no longer waltzes, but he 'participates in round dances;' he is not thanked, but he is 'the recipient of grateful acknowledgments.' A home is not building, but is 'in process of erection;' it is not burned down, but is 'destroyed in its entirety by the devouring element.' A ship is not launched, but it 'glides into its native element.' When a man narrowly escapes drowning, 'the waves are balked of their prey.' Not only presidents, but aqueducts, millinery shops, and railroad strikes are 'inaugurated.' We no longer threaten, but we 'indulge in minatory expressions.' This vulgar finery is so much worn in the pulpit as to render plain language there offensive. An American clergyman was subjected to a severe censure for using the word 'beans' in a sermon; and a recent English magazine relates a similar incident: 'I remember quite a sensation running through a congregation when a preacher one evening, instead of talking about 'habits of cleanliness' and the 'necessity of regular ablution,' remarked that 'plenty of water had a healthy, bracing effect upon the body, and so indirectly benefited the mind.'"

We refer the student to Macaulay's "History of England" as a model of clear style and almost perfect choice of words. 'A study of this work will do much to impart clearness and to cure one of the faults of ambiguity and obscurity.

CHAPTER VII.

THE CHOICE OF WORDS (CONTINUED)

THE SECOND essential in the choice of words is *force, or strength*. In certain forms of composition, as for instance judicial opinions, scientific reports, text-books and other forms of writing, the purpose of which is simply to furnish instruction or information, clearness is the prime essential, and force is not so much needed. But in writing or speaking, the purpose of which is to *impress* and influence the minds of others, force and strength are required. The words must be chosen not only with the idea and purpose of clearness but also with the direct intent to attract and hold the attention of the person addressed, and to make him *feel* the meaning behind the words. Force is needed to attract attention, to arouse interest, to awaken desire, and to cause action. This quality of force or strength is known by different names among the authorities. Campbell calls it *vivacity*; Whately, *energy*; Bain, *strength*; but as Hill says: "a style may be vivacious without being energetic, or energetic without being strong. *Force* covers the ground more satisfactorily, perhaps, than any other single term."

In choosing words for their quality of force, it will be found that in the majority of cases the *clearest* word will prove the most forcible. But when the choice is between two words equally clear, it will be found that one or the other seems to possess an illustrative force superior to the other. This arises from a peculiar psychological association, and is recognized more or less instinctively, once the attention is directed toward the subject. The speaker *feels* the force of the word, as does the hearer. As an illustration of the comparative force of words, let us direct your attention to the following familiar quotation— the Parable of the Lilies—and then to the paraphrase of a modern writer designed to bring out this particular point. The Parable follows:

> "Consider the lilies how they grow; they toll not, they spin not; and; yet I say unto you, that Solomon in all his glory was not arrayed like one of these. If then God so clothe the grass which is to-day in the field, and to-morrow is cast into the oven, how much more will he clothe you, O ye of little faith!"—LUKE xii: 27, 28.

Campbell, referring to the Parable just quoted, says: "Let us here adopt a little of the tasteless manner of modern paraphrase by the substitution of more general terms, one of their many expedients of infrigidating, and let us observe the effect produced by this change: 'Consider the flowers, how they continually increase in their size; they do no manner of work, and yet I declare to you that no king whatever, in his most splendid habit, is dressed up like them. If, then, God in His providence both so adorn the vegetable productions, which continue but a little time on the land, and are afterwards put into the fire, how much more will He provide clothing for you!'" Hill, commenting on this well-known paraphrase, says: "In this paraphrase, the thought is expressed as clearly as in the original, and more exactly; but the comparison, in the original, between a common flower and the most magnificent of kings is much more impressive than any general statement can be; and the mind, without conscious exertion, understands that what is true of the lily as compared with Solomon is true of all flowers as compared with all men."

In considering the element of *force* in the choice of words, we are compelled to take into account the forcible effect of the *figures of speech* of rhetoric, but we shall not mention them at this place as they will form the subject of a subsequent chapter.

The quality of *suggestion* in words adds materially to their force. Words whose sounds suggest their meaning are forceful for this reason. Hill says: "Force may be gained by the use of words of which the sound suggests the meaning. Such are words denoting sounds: *whiz, roar, splash, thud, buzz, hubbub, murmur, hiss, rattle, boom*; names taken from sounds: *cuckoo, whip-poor-will, bumble-bee, humming bird, crag*; words so arranged that the sound expresses the meaning:

"* * * On a sudden open fly
With impetuous recoil and jarring sound
Th' infernal doors, and on their hinges grate harsh thunder."
"And the long carpets rose along the gusty floor."
"On the ear
Drops the light drip of the suspended oar,
And chirps the grasshopper one good-night carol more."

"Such are many interjections: *heigh-ho! whew! hist! bang! ding-dong! pooh! hush!* Such, too, are words derived from objects of the senses, but applied to mental phenomena because of a supposed resemblance or association of ideas: 'a *harsh* temper,' '*soft* manner,' 'a *sweet* disposition,' '*stormy* passions,' 'a *quick* mind,' 'a *sharp* tongue.' Such words, or combinations of words, have certain obvious advantages. They are not only specific, clear and forcible, but also so familiar that they may be accounted natural symbols rather than arbitrary signs; but they may be misused, as when chosen with an obvious effort, or because they sound well, rather than because they are peculiarly expressive. The safe course is, on the one hand, not to reject a word or phrase because its sound helps to communicate the meaning; on the other hand, not to strain after such expressions, lest, in the effort to grasp the shadow, the substance is lost."

Notice the suggestive force of the following passage from Tennyson, the words of which impress upon one with an almost weird effect the silent old house, its dim uncanny reminiscent atmosphere of the past, its mysterious spirit of the by-gone presences which haunt the old scenes:

"All day within the dreary house
　　The doors upon their hinges creaked,
The blue fly sang in the pane, the mouse
　　Behind the mouldering wainscoat shrieked,
Or from the crevice peered about;
　　Old faces glimmered thro' the doors,
　　Old footsteps trod the upper floors,
Old voices called her from without."

The following quotations will also give the student an idea of the powerfully suggestive effective effect of words and arrangement of words. We give these examples for the purpose of enabling the student to grasp the actual effect of suggestive words and sentences, believing that the idea may be better grasped in this way than by the attempt to follow any arbitrary rule. It is most difficult to enunciate a rule in this case—example and imitation work the best results. Listening to the conversation of a strong speaker, or reading the speeches of the best orators, Will do more to form the idea of *force* in the mind of the student than would pages of arbitrary rules or general advice. Read the following quotations slowly and carefully, endeavoring to *feel* the *suggestive force* of the words, and in the associations called forth by the arrangement:

ILLUSTRATIVE EXAMPLES.

"Over it rose the noisy belfry of the College, the square, brown tower of the church, and the slim, yellow spire of the parish meeting-house, by no means ungraceful, and then an invariable characteristic of New England religious architecture. On your right, the Charles slipped smoothly through green and purple salt meadows, darkened, here and there, with the blossoming black-grass as with a stranded cloud-shadow. Over these marshes, level as water, but without its glare, and with softer and more soothing gradations of perspective, the eye was carried to a horizon of softly-rounded hills. To your left hand, upon the Old Road, you saw some half-dozen dignified old houses of the colonial time, all comfortably fronting southward. If it were early June, the rows of horse-chestnuts along the fronts of these houses showed through every crevice of their dark heap of foliage, and on the end of every drooping limb, a cone of pearly flowers, while the hill behind was white or rosy with the crowding blooms of various fruit trees. There is no sound, unless a horseman clatters over the loose planks of the bridge, while his antipodal shadow glides silently over the mirrored bridge below."—LOWELL: *Cambridge Thirty Years Ago.*

"There was in the court a peculiar silence somehow; and the scene remained long in Esmond's memory:—the sky bright overhead; the buttresses of the building and the sun-dial casting shadow over the gilt *memento mori* inscribed underneath; the two dogs, a black greyhound and a spaniel nearly white, the one with his face up to the sun, and the other snuffing amongst the grass and stones, and my lord leaning over the fountain, which was bubbling audibly.

"How well all things were remembered! The ancient towers and gables of the ball darkling against the east, the purple shadows on the green slopes, the quaint devices and carvings of the dial, the forest-crowned heights, the fair, yellow plain cheerful with crops and corn, the shining river rolling through it towards the pearly hills beyond,—all these were before us, along with a thousand beautiful memories of our youth, beautiful and sad, but as real and vivid in our minds as that fair and always-remembered scene our eyes beheld once more."—THACKERAY: Henry Esmond.

"It was an exquisite January morning in which there was no threat of rain, but a grey sky making the calmest back-ground for the charms of a mild winter scene:—the grassy borders of the lanes, the hedge-rows sprinkled with red berries and haunted with low twitterings, the purple bareness of the elms, the rich brown of the furrows."—GEORGE ELIOT: Daniel Deronda.

"So much describes the stuffy little room.
Vulgar, flat, smooth respectability:
Not so the burst of landscape surging in,
Sunrise and all, as he who of the pair
Is, plain enough, the younger personage
Draws sharp the shrieking curtain, sends aloft
The sash, spreads wide and fastens back to wall
Shutter and shutter, shows you England's best.
He leans into a living glory-bath
Of air and light, where seems to float and move
The wooded, watered country, hill and dale
And steel-bright thread of stream, a-smoke with mist,
A-sparkle with May morning, diamond drift
O' the sun-touched dew."—BROWNING: The Inn Album.

"Night Is a dead, monotonous period under a roof; but in the open world it passes lightly, with its stars and dews and perfumes, and the hours are marked by changes in the face of Nature. What seems a kind of temporal death to people choked between walls and curtains, is only a light and living slumber to the man who sleeps afield. All night long he can hear Nature breathing deeply and freely; even as she takes her rest she turns and smiles; and there is one stirring hour unknown to those who dwell in houses when a wakeful influence goes abroad over the sleeping hemisphere, and all the out-door world are on their feet. It is then that the cock first crows, not this time to announce the dawn, but like a cheerful watchman speeding the course of night. Cattle awake on the meadows; sheep break their fast on dewy hillsides, and change to a new lair among the ferns; and houseless men, who have lain down with the fowls, open their dim eyes and behold the beauty of the night."—STEVENSON: *Travels with a Donkey*.

"Pathetic little tumble-down old houses, all out of drawing and perspective, nestled like old spiders' webs between the buttresses of the great cathedral."—DU MAURIER: *Trilby*.

"The light seemed to go out of his eyes and leave them like stale opals."—KIPLING: *The Second Jungle-Book*.

"The fog was driven apart for a moment, and the sun shone, a blood-red wafer, on the water."—KIPLING: *Plain Tales from the Hills*.

"The aftermath of the dust storm came up and drove us down-wind like pieces of paper,"—IBID.

"But the walls were made of screens of marble tracery—beautiful, milk-white fretwork, set with agates and carnelians and jasper and lapis lazuli, and as the moon came up behind the hill it shone through the openwork, casting shadows on the ground like black-velvet embroidery."—KIPLING: *The Jungle-Book*.

"The feeling of unhappiness he had never known before covered him as water covers a log."—KIPLING: *The Second Jungle-Book*.

"The traveller, descending from the slopes of Luna, even as he got his first view of the Port-of-Venus, would pause by the way, to read the face as it were, of so beautiful a dwelling place, lying away from the white road, at the point where it began to decline somewhat steeply to the marsh-land below. The building of pale red and yellow marble, mellowed by age, which he saw beyond the gates, was indeed but the exquisite fragment of a once large and sumptuous villa. Two centuries of the play of the sea-wind were in the velvet of the mosses which lay along its inaccessible ledges and angles. Here and there the marble plates had slipped from their places, where the delicate weeds had forced their way. The graceful wildness which prevailed in garden and farm gave place to a singular nicety about the actual habitation, and a still more scrupulous sweetness and order reigned within."—PATER: *Marius the Epicurean*.

"About six miles from the renowned city of the Manhattoes, in that sound or arm of the sea which passes between the mainland and Nassau, or Long Island, there is a narrow strait, where the current is violently compressed between shouldering promontories and horribly perplexed rocks and shoals. Being, at the best of times, a very violent, impetuous current, it takes these impediments in mighty dudgeon, boiling in whirlpools; brawling and fretting in ripples; raging and roaring in rapids and breakers; and, in short, indulging in all sorts of wrong-headed paroxysms. At such times, woe to any unlucky vessel that ventures within its clutches. This termagant humor, however, prevails only at certain times of tide. At low water, for instance, it is as pacific a stream as you would wish to see; but as the tide rises it begins to fret; at half tide it roars with might and main like a bull bellowing for more drink; but when the tide is full it relapses into quiet, and, for a time, sleeps as soundly as an alderman after dinner."—IRVING.

"The morning broke with sinister brightness; the air alarmingly transparent, the sky pure, the rim of the horizon clear and strong against the heavens. The wind and the wild seas, now vastly swollen, indefatigably hunted us. I stood on deck, choking with fear; I seemed to lose all power upon my limbs; my knees were as paper when she plunged into the murderous valleys; my heart collapsed when some black mountain fell in avalanche beside her counter, and the water, that was more than spray, swept round my ankles like a torrent. I was conscious of but one strong desire, to bear myself decently in my terrors, and whatever should happen to my life, preserve my character: as the captain said, we are a queer kind of beasts. Breakfast time came, and I made shift to swallow some hot tea. Then I must stagger below to take the time, reading the chronometer with dizzy eyes, and marveling the while what value there could be in observations taken in a ship launched (as ours then was) like a missile among flying seas. The forenoon dragged on in a grinding monotony of peril; every spoke of the wheel a rash, but an obliged experiment—rash as a forlorn hope, needful as the leap that lands a fireman from a burning staircase. Noon was made; the captain dined on his day's work, and I on watching him; and our place was entered on the chart with a meticulous precision which seemed half pitiful and half absurd, since the next eye to behold that sheet of paper might be the eye of an exploring fish. One o'clock came, then two; the captain gloomed and chafed, as he held to the coaming of the house, and if ever I saw dormant murder in man's eye, it was in his. God help the hand that should have disobeyed him."—STEVENSON: *The Wrecker.*

CHAPTER VIII.

FIGURATIVE SPEECH

QUACKENBOS SAYS: "Figurative Language implies a departure from the simple or ordinary mode of expression; a clothing of ideas in words which not only convey the meaning, but, through a comparison or some other means of exciting the imagination, convey it in such a way as to make a lively and forcible impression on the mind. Thus, if we say: 'Saladin was shrewd in the council, braw in the field,' we express the thought in the simplest manner. But if we vary the expression thus: 'Saladin was a fox in the council, a lion in the field,' we clothe the same sentiment in figurative language. Instead of cunning and courage, iWe introduce the animals that possess these qualities in the highest degree, and thus present livelier images to the mind."

What are known as "figures of rhetoric" are the numerous individuals of a large class of language forms, the characteristic quality of which is deviation from the ordinary, plain and practical application of words. We find them everywhere in all forms of verbal expression. They give beauty, life and strength to style, and, as Scott says: "it would perhaps be truer to say that *they have the power of arousing in the reader or hearer the same emotional and imaginative processes which gave birth to them in the mind of the writer.*" In other words, they are powerful instruments or agents of *suggestion.*

Rhetoricians have devoted much time, attention and space to the task of analyzing, defining and classifying the various rhetorical figures. By refining the definitions and classification, some authorities have succeeded in enumerating nearly three hundred classes of rhetorical figures. Such classification is, however, of but little practical value to the general student. The modern text. books generally confine themselves to a consideration of not over ten or twelve of the more important classes. The following are the more important Rhetorical Figures of Imagery:

I. *Metaphor,* or "a figure of speech by which a word is transferred from an object to which it properly belongs to another, in such a manner that a comparison is implied though not formally expressed." Thus: "He is a tiger," or "She is a cat." There is a close resemblance between a *metaphor* and a *simile,* the difference consisting of words implying comparison, such as "like" or "as." For instance: "He is a fox," is a *metaphor*; while, "He is *like* a fox" is a *simile.* It will be seen, therefore, that every metaphor may be converted into a simile by extension; and that every simile may be converted into a metaphor, by condensation.

Hill says: "All writers agree that, other things being equal, the metaphor is more forcible than the simile; but opinions differ as to the true explanation of the fact. According to Dr. Whateley, who adopts the idea from Aristotle, the superiority of the metaphor is ascribable to the fact that 'all men are more gratified at catching the resemblance for themselves, than at having it pointed out for them;' according to Herbert Spencer, 'the great economy it achieves would seem to be the more probable cause:' but neither explanation is altogether satisfactory." The following quotation will give a general idea of the metaphor and the simile, combined and contrasted in the same paragraph:

"Some minds are wonderful for keeping their bloom in this way, as a *patriarchal gold-fish* apparently retains to the last its youthful illusion that it can swim in a straight line beyond the encircling glass. Mrs. Tulliver *was an amiable fish* of this kind; and, after running her head against the same resisting medium for thirteen years, would go at it again to-day with undulled alacrity."—GEORGE ELIOT: *Mill on the Floss*.

Writers and speakers frequently employ metaphors containing two or more images which are incongruous and which fail to blend—these are called "mixed metaphors." The incongruous figurative jumble arising from the use of the mixed metaphor is frequently amusing and always ludicrous. For instance the old "bull:" "Every time he *opens his mouth, he puts his foot in it*;" or: "With swift *rapier-thrusts* of irony, the prosecuting attorney *applied the thumbscrews* to the unwilling witness." Or the famous instance of Dickens, who said, speaking of the street lamps: "At night, when the lamplighter had let these down, and lighted and hoisted them again, a feeble *grove* of dim wicks swung in a *sickly* manner overhead, as if they were *at sea*." Or that of De Quincy who said: "the howling *wilderness* of the psalmody in most parish churches of the land *countersigns* the statement." Or, "Boyle was the *father of chemistry* and *brother to the Earl of Cork*." Or "A *torrent* of superstition *consumed* the land." Or, "Trothal went forth with the *stream* of his people, but they met a rock: for Fingal stood unmoved; broken, they rolled back from his side. Nor did they *roll* in safety; the spear of the king pursued their *flight*."

II. *Allegory*, or "A discourse designed to convey a different meaning from that which it directly expresses; a figure of speech in which the speaker or writer gives forth not only the actual narrative, description, or whatever he wishes to present, but one so much resembling it as on reflection to suggest it, and bring home to the mind with greater force and effect than if it had been told directly." An *allegory* is really an *extended metaphor*. An allegory may be short, brief and pointed, in which case it is known as a "fable" or "parable." The fables of Æsop, and the Parables of the Bible, are forms of allegory. Bunyan's "Pilgrim's Progress" is probably the best example of extended allegory. Spencer's "Faerie Queen" is a moral allegory. Macaulay says: "Bunyan is indeed as decidedly the first of allegorists, as Demosthenes is the first of orators, or Shakespeare the first of dramatists." The following is an example of a brief allegory:

> "Thou hast brought a vine out of Egypt. Thou hast cast out the heathen, and planted it. Thou preparedst room before it, and didst cause it to take deep root, and it filled the land. The hills were covered with the shadow of it, and the boughs thereof were like the goodly cedars."

III. *Simile*, or "the likening of two things, which though differing in many respects, have some strong point or points of resemblance." We have explained the distinction between the *metaphor* and the *simile*. In the metaphor the resemblance between the original object and the adopted image is *boldly assumed*; while in the *simile* the resemblance is *formally stated* by the words "as" or "like." The Songs of Solomon are filled with beautiful similes. The following from Ossian is an example of the use of the simile:

> "Pleasant are the words of the song, said Cuchullin, and lovely are the tales of other times. They are like the calm dew of the morning on the hill of roes, when the sun is faint on its side, and the lake is settled and blue in the vale."

IV. *Synecdoche*, or "a figure of speech by which the whole of a thing is taken for the part, or a part for the whole, as the genus for the species, or the species for the genus." As for example: "All *hands* on deck;" "The sea is covered with *sails*;" "Our *hero* was gray, but not from age;" "Ten thousand. were *on his right hand*."

V. *Metonymy*, or "a figure of speech by which one word is put or used for another; as when the effect is substituted for the cause; the inventor for the thing invented; the material for the thing made; etc." For example we say, "He keeps a good *table*;" or "We read *Virgil*;" or "The poorest man in his cottage may bid defiance to all the force of *the Crown*;" or "He petitioned *the Bench*, being a member of *the Bar*." There is a very, close resemblance between *metonymy* and *synecdoche*.

In addition to the above-mentioned Rhetorical Figures of Imagery, there are several Rhetorical Figures of Arrangement, in which words, phrases, clauses, sentences, figures, etc., are arranged in a peculiar or striking way. The principal Figures of Arrangement are as follows:

I. *Climax*, or "a figure in which the sense rises gradually step by step in a series of images, each exceeding its predecessor in force and dignity," or "the arrangement of a succession of words, clauses, or sentences, in such a way that the weakest may stand first, and that each in turn, to the end, may rise in importance, and make a deeper impression on the mind than that which preceded it. As for example: "It is an outrage to bind a Roman citizen; it is a crime to scourge him; it is almost parricide to kill him; but to crucify him—what shall I say of this?" or, "Who shall separate us from the love of Christ? Shall tribulation, or distress, or persecution, or famine, or nakedness, or peril, or sword?"

II. *Antithesis*, or "sharp opposition between word and word, clause and clause, sentence and sentence, or sentiment and sentiment, specially designed to impress the reader or hearer." As for example: "He had *covertly shot at Cromwell*, he now *openly aimed at the Queen*;" "To *err* is human, to *forgive* divine;" "Though *grave*, yet *trifling*; *zealous*, yet *untrue*." Its importance as an . effective instrument of expression is admitted by all the authorities. As the author of Lacon says: "To extirpate antithesis from literature altogether, would be to destroy at one stroke about eight-tenths of all the wit, ancient and modern, now existing in the world."

III. *Irony*, or "a mode of speech in which the meaning is contrary to the words. The intention is mildly to ridicule undue pretensions or absurd statements while nominally accepting them unquestionably." In *irony*, the real meaning is subtly suggested by the tone of the voice or the implication of the words. As for example when Elijah said to the priests of Baal, who were endeavoring to persuade their god to manifest himself in a miraculous manner: "Cry aloud, for he is a *god*. Either he is talking, or he is pursuing, or he is on a journey, or peradventure he sleepeth, and must be awakened I"

IV. *Epigram*, or "a sentence of brief and pointed character." As for example Talleyrand's famous saying: "Language was given to man to conceal his thoughts." The epigram is often used with great effect, even when it implies a fallacy. Many people accept a snappy, pointed statement, cleverly phrased, as a self-evident truth—they delude themselves into believing that the *epigram* is an *axiom*. For this reason, and because it adds brilliancy and sparkle to a discourse, many speakers employ the epigram very freely.

V. *Hyperbole*, or "the figure of speech which depends upon exaggeration for its effect." Blair says: "It consists in magnifying an object beyond its natural bounds. In all languages, even in common conversation, hyperbolical expressions very frequently occur; as 'swift as the wind;' 'as white as the snow;' and the like; and our common forms of compliment are almost all of them extravagant hyperboles." Hyperbole is an inheritance from the Oriental writers, who indulge in it freely. It is a characteristic of the young writer or speaker, and often arises from a lively imagination which generally finds pleasure in magnifying things. Hyperbole also often results from an ardent temperament or aroused emotion, although it may also be caused by a keen sense of humor, in which case it takes on the attributes of *irony*. In addition to the examples given above, the following will serve to illustrate this figure of speech: "Saul and Jonathan were *swifter than eagles*, and *stronger than lions*."

"And trembling Tiber *dived beneath his bed.*" "*Swifter than the winds* and *the wings of the lightning.*"

VI. *Vision,* or "the representation of past events, or imaginary objects and scenes, as actually present to the senses." As for example: "Cæsar *leaves* Gaul *crosses* the Rubicon, and *enters* Italy;" or "They *rally,* they *bleed,* for their kingdom and crown." The effect of the figure is produced by the substitution of the present tense for the past.

VII. *Apostrophe,* or "the turning from the regular course of the subject, into an invocation or address." As for example: "Death is swallowed up in victory. O, death, where is thy sting? O, grave, where is thy victory?" It has the effect of turning aside from the auditor or audience and addressing some abstract principle, inanimate object, or person not present.

VIII. *Personification,* or "the attributing of sex, life, or action to an inanimate object, or the ascribing of intelligence and personality to an inferior creature." As for example: "The sea *saw it* and *fled;*" or, "The worm, *aware* of his intent, *harangued* him thus."

IX. *Interrogation,* or "the asking of questions, not ·for the purpose of expressing doubt or obtaining information, but in order:to assert strongly the reverse of what is asked." As for example: "Doth God pervert judgment? or doth the Almighty pervert justice?" The employment of this figure imparts life and animation. The Book of Job gives us one of the best examples of its effective use.

X. *Exclamation,* or "the expression of some strong emotion for the purpose of impression." As for example: "Oh! the depth of the riches both of the wisdom and the knowledge of God!"

XI. *Omission,* or "the pretended suppression or omission of what one is actually mentioning all the time." As for example: "*I say nothing* of the notorious profligacy of his character; *nothing* of the reckless extravagance with which he has wasted an ample fortune; *nothing* of the disgusting intemperance which has sometimes caused him to reel in our streets—but I aver that he has exhibited neither probity nor ability in the important office which he holds."

XII. *Euphemism*, or "the use of a delicate word or expression for one which is harsh, indelicate or offensive to delicate ears." As for example: "*Intoxicated*" for "drunk;" "*passed away*" or "*passed out*" for" died;" "*casket*" for "coffin;" "*misappropriated property*" for "embezzled;" "*a disciple of Bacchus*" for "a drunkard;" "*a votary at the shrine of Venus*" for "a libertine;" "*limb*" for "leg;" "*vest*" for "undershirt; " etc.

Of the above rhetorical figures, four (metaphor, metonymy, synecdoche, and irony) and often more, are frequently called "*tropes*." A *Trope* is: "a figurative use of a word; a word or expression used in a different sense from that which it properly possesses, or a word changed from its original signification to another for the sake of giving life or emphasis to an idea, as when we call a stupid fellow an ass, or a shrewd man a fox." Blair says: "Figures of words are commonly called *tropes*, and consist in a word's being employed to signify something that is different from its original and primitive, so that if you alter the word, you destroy the figure."

Carlyle says of figures of speech: "Thinkest thou there were no poets till Dan Chaucer? No heart burning with a thought, which it could not hold, and had no word for; and needed to shape and coin a word for,—what thou callest a metaphor, trope, or the like? For every word we have, there was such a man and poet. The coldest word was once a glowing new metaphor, and bold questionable originality. 'Thy very *Attention*, does it not mean an *attentio, a stretching-to*?' Fancy that act of the mind, which all were conscious of, which none had yet named,— when this new 'poet' first felt bound and driven to name it! His questionable originality, and new glowing metaphor, was found adoptable, intelligible; and remains our name for it to this day."

CHAPTER IX.

DISCOURSIVE EXPRESSION

THE VERB "to discourse" means: "To treat of; to talk over; to discuss; to relate; to debate; to reason; to pass from premises to consequences; to treat upon anything in a formal manner by words; to dilate; to hold forth; to expatiate; etc." "Discoursive" of course means: "Of, or pertaining to reasoning or discourse." By Discoursive Expression is meant the expression of one's ideas or thoughts in the form of discourse.

The authorities recognize four distinct forms or phases of Discoursive Expression; viz., (1) Descriptive Discourse; (2) Narrative Discourse; (3). Expositive Discourse; and (4) Argumentive Discourse. *Descriptive Discourse* is that form of discourse in which the attributes, properties, qualities and relations of persons or things are explained in the form of a representation of them as they appear in the mind of the speaker. *Narrative Discourse* is that form of discourse in which acts or events are related in the form of a story. *Expositive Discourse* is that form of discourse in which the subject or object is analyzed and explained in detail, and definitely. *Argumentive Discourse* is that form of discourse in which an effort is made to so present the subject as to influence the opinion and understanding of the hearer, and to move his will.

Descriptive Discourse deals with the *explanation* of persons or things. "Description" means: "The act of describing, defining, or setting forth the qualities, characteristics, properties or features, of anything in words, so as to convey an idea of it to another." In order to *describe* a thing we must state its various properties, qualities, attributes and relations. In order to do this, we must first analyze or "take apart" the thing itself—we must view it in its parts as well as a whole. We must be able to take the thing apart, mentally, and then put it together again. As Coleridge says: "Description seems to be like taking the pieces of a dissected map out of its box. We first look at one part and then at another, then join and dovetail them, and when the successive acts of attention have been completed, there is a retrogressive effort of mind to behold it as a whole."

Descriptive Discourse may be divided into two general classes, viz., (a) Analytical Description; and (b) General Description.

In *Analytical Description*, the various parts, qualities, attributes, properties, etc., are considered and explained separately and apart, and without reference to each other or to the whole. In other words, the various items composing and constituting the whole thing are *catalogued separately*. This form of description is met with in technical and scientific discourse, and to a certain extent in legal statements. The "specifications" for the building of a house; the scientific description of an animal; the legal statement of the details of a patent, description of a piece of real estate, etc., give us examples of this form of description. The following Analytical Description of the Barn Swallow, given by Prof. Edward A. Samuels, will give an excellent example of this form of description:

> "BARN SWALLOW (*Hirundo horreorum*): Tail very deeply forked; outer feather of tail several inches longer than the inner, very narrow towards the end; above glossy-blue, with concealed white in the middle of the back; throat chestnut; rest of lower part reddish-white, not conspicuously different; a steel-blue collar on the upper part of the

breast, interrupted in the middle; tail feathers with a white spot near the middle, on the inner web. Female with the outer tail feathers not quite so long. Length, six and ninety one-hundredths inches; wing, five inches; tail, four and fifty one-hundredths inches."

In *General Description*, the thing is considered as a whole, the general appearance being considered and explained. For instance, in the case of a *house*, the general appearance, shape, position, location, color, style of architecture, size, probable cost, general effect, etc., would be considered and described, without regard to the details of Construction contained in the "specification" which were considered in detail in the Analytical Description. In the case of the *barn-swallow*, the general appearance of the bird, its peculiar wings and long tail, its graceful flight, its color, its nest and dwelling-place, would be considered instead of the technical, scientific description made necessary in a scientific Analytical Description such as quoted above from Prof. Samuels.

General Description may be either *literal* or *impressional*. By *literal description* is meant a description "according to the primitive meaning or letter; not figurative or metaphorical; formally, plainly and clearly expressed." By *impressional description* is meant a description in metaphor or other figure of speech, or else by means of suggestive terms which give the outlines and excite the imagination to fill in the picture. The term arises from "Impressionism," which is defined as: "The system in art or literature, which, avoiding elaboration, seeks to depict scenes in nature as they are first vividly impressed on the mind of the artist or writer."

Literal description appeals to the intellect; impressional description appeals to the imagination. We have familiar examples of literal description in business conversation and correspondence, and in ordinary newspaper writing. Examples of impressional description are given in our preceding chapters in which figures of speech are considered. Dickens and Thackeray were masters of this form of description. The following from Dickens furnishes an excellent example:

> "'A slight figure,' said Mr. Peggotty, looking at the fire, 'kiender worn; soft, sorrowful, blue eyes; a delicate face; a pritty head, leaning a little down; a quiet voice and way—timid a'most. That's Em'ly! * * * * Cheerful along with me; retired when others is by; fond of going any distance fur to teach a child, or fur to tend a sick person, or fur to do some kindness tow'rds a young girl's wedding (and she's done a many, but has never seen one); fondly loving of her uncle; patient; liked by young and old; sowt out by all that has any trouble. That's Em'ly!'"

Narrative Discourse deals with the *telling* the story of acts or events—the relating of the *history* of an occurrence. "Narrate" means "to tell, or relate; to recite or rehearse as a story, etc." Narrative Description, also, may be either (a) *literal;* or (b) *impressional*, the definitions given under the head of "Description" applying equally in this case. And in the same way, Narrative Discourse may be considered in its phases of (a) *analytical;* and (b) *general;* according to its nature. Hyslop says: "Narration is that process of explanation which presents a theme *in its time relations*, or which exhibits events in their proper order. * * * In pure mathematical narration the principle must be in chronological order. In pure logical narration the principle must be logical classification and connection of events without regard to other events in the same time. In many instances, however, it is possible and will be proper to combine both processes. This may be done in various degrees according as the object of the narration permits it."

Hill makes the following valuable comments upon Narrative Discourse: "As the main purpose of narration is to tell a story, a narrative should move from the beginning to the end, and it should move with method. A narrative may move rapidly * * * or slowly * * * but *movement* it must have. * * * Every story, whether it moves swiftly or slowly, is successful or unsuccessful as a narrative according as it is or is not interrupted. * * * It is not enough that a narrative should move; it should move forward, it should have *method*. * * * A narrator fails as a narrator in so far as he does not go straight on from the beginning to the end. A story teller who runs this way and that in pursuit of something which is entirely aside from his narrative, and who returns to his subject as if by accident, is perhaps the most vexatious of all who try to communicate by language with their fellow beings. * * * To secure method in movement, a writer (or speaker) should keep constantly in mind the central idea of his narrative; about that central idea he should group all other ideas according to their relative value and pertinence."

The student will do well to read the stories of Kipling, Poe, Hawthorne, and Maupassant in order to "catch" the spirit of the true narrative style. Some of Richard Harding Davis's short stories are well adapted for such study. And Stevenson, of course, will ever be worthy of study, analysis, and of great value as a model of narrative style. The following from Stevenson's "Will o' the Mill" will give an idea of the strength and simplicity of his style. Describing the final scene in the life of the old "Will" who from boyhood had dwelt in the old mill, preaching and practicing his quaint philosophy of life, he says:

"One night, in his seventy-second year, he awoke in bed, in such uneasiness of body and mind that he arose and dressed himself and went out to meditate in the arbor. It was pitch dark, without a star; the river was swollen, and the wet woods and meadows loaded the air with perfume. It had thundered during the day, and it promised more thunder for the morrow. A murky, stifling night for a man of seventy-two! Whether it was the weather or the wakefulness, or some little touch of fever in his old limbs, Will's mind was besieged by tumultuous and crying memories. His boyhood, the night with the fat young man, the death of his adopted parents, the summer days with Marjory, and many of those small circumstances which seem nothing to another, and are yet the very gist of a man's own life to himself,—

things seen, words heard, looks misconstrued—arose from their forgotten corners and usurped his attention. The dead themselves were with him, not merely taking part in this thin show of memory that defiled before his brain, but revisiting his bodily senses as they do in profound and vivid dreams. The fat young man leaned his elbows on the table opposite; Marjory came and went with an apronful of flowers between the garden and the arbor; he could bear the old parson knocking out his pipe or blowing his resonant nose. The tide of his consciousness ebbed and flowed: He was sometimes half asleep and drowned in his recollections of the past; and sometimes he was broad awake, wondering at himself.

"But about the middle of the night he was startled by the voice of the dead miller calling to him out of the house as he used to do on the arrival of custom. The hallucination was so perfect that Will sprang from his seat and stood listening for the summons to be repeated; and as he listened he became conscious of another noise besides the brawling of the river and the ringing in his feverish ears. It was like the stir of the horses and the creaking of harness, as though a carriage with an impatient team had been brought up upon the road before the courtyard gate. At such an hour, upon this rough and dangerous pass, the supposition was no better than absurd; and Will dismissed it from his mind, and resumed his seat upon the arbor chair; and sleep closed over him again like running water. He was once again awakened by the dead miller's call, thinner and more spectral than before; and once again he heard the noise of an equipage upon the road. And so thrice and four times the same dream, or the same fancy, presented itself to his senses, until at length, smiling to himself as when one humors a nervous child, he proceeded towards the gate to set his uncertainty at rest.

"From the arbor to the gate was no great distance, and yet it took Will some time; it seemed as if the dead thickened around him in the court, and crossed his path at every step. For, first, he was suddenly surprised by an overpowering sweetness of heliotropes; it was as if his garden had been planted with this flower from end to end, and the hot damp night had drawn forth all their perfumes in a breath. Now the heliotrope had been Marjory's favorite flower, and since her death not one of them had ever been planted in Will's ground. 'I must be going crazy,' he thought. 'Poor Marjory and her heliotropes!' And with that he raised his eyes towards the window that had once been hers. If he had been bewildered before, he was now almost terrified; for there was a light in the room; the window was an orange oblong as of yore; and the corner of the blind was lifted and let fall as on the night when he stood and shouted to the stars in his perplexity. The illusion only endured an instant; but it left him somewhat unmanned, rubbing his eyes, and staring at the outline of the house and the black night behind it. While he thus stood, and it seemed as if he must have stood there quite a long time, there came a renewal of the noises on the road; and he turned in time to meet a stranger, who was advancing to meet him across the court. There was something like the outline of a great carriage discernible on the road behind the stranger, and, above that, a few black pine-tops, like so many plumes. 'Master Will?' asked the newcomer in brief, military fashion. 'That same, sir,' answered Will. 'Can I do anything to serve you?' 'I have heard you much spoken of, Master Will,' returned the other; 'much spoken of, and well. And, although I have both bands full of business. I wish to drink a bottle of wine with you in your arbor. Before I go I shall introduce myself.'

"Will led the way to the trellis, and got a lamp lighted, and a bottle uncorked. He was not altogether unused to such complimentary interviews, and hoped little enough from this one, being schooled in many disappointments. A sort of cloud had settled on his wits and prevented him from remembering the strangeness of the hour. He moved like a person in his sleep; and it seemed as if the lamp caught fire and the bottle came uncorked with the facility of thought. Still, he had some curiosity about the appearance of his visitor, and tried in vain to turn the light into his face; either he handled the light clumsily, or there was a dimness over his eyes; but he could make out little more than a shadow at table with him. He stared and stared at this shadow, as he wiped out the glasses, and began to feel cold and strange about the heart. The silence weighed upon him; for he could hear nothing now, not even the river, but the drumming of his own arteries in his ears.

"'Here's to you,' said the stranger roughly. 'Here is my service, sir,' replied Will sipping his wine, which somehow tasted oddly. 'I understand you are a very positive fellow,' pursued the stranger. Will made answer with a smile of some satisfaction and a little nod. 'So am I,' continued the other, 'and it is the delight of my heart to tramp on people's corns. I will have nobody positive but myself; not one. I have crossed the whims, in my time, of kings and generals and great artists. And what would you say,' he went on, 'If I had come up here on purpose to cross yours.' Will had it on his tongue to make a sharp rejoinder; but the politeness of the old innkeeper prevailed, and he held his peace and made answer with a civil gesture of the hand 'I have,' said the stranger. 'And If I did not hold you in a particular esteem, I should make no words about the matter. It appears you pride yourself on staying where you are. You mean to stick by your inn. Now I mean you shall come for a turn with me in my barouche; and before this bottle's empty, so you shall.' 'That would be an odd thing, to be sure,' replied Will with a chuckle. 'Why, sir, I have grown here like an old oak tree; the Devil himself could hardly root me up; and for all I perceive you are a very entertaining old gentleman, I would wager you another bottle you lose your pains with me.' The dimness of Will's eyesight had been increasing all this while; but he was somewhat conscious of a sharp and chilling scrutiny which irritated and yet overwhelmed him. 'You need not think,' he broke out suddenly, in an explosive, febrile manner which startled and alarmed himself, 'that I am a stay-at-home, because I fear anything under God. God knows I am tired enough of it all; and when the time comes for a longer journey than ever you dream of, I reckon I shall find myself prepared.' The stranger emptied his glass and pushed it away from him. He looked down for a little, and then, leaning over the table, tapped Will three times upon the forearm with a single finger. 'The time has come,' he said solemnly.

"An ugly thrill spread from the spot be touched. The tones of his voice were dull and startling, and echoed strangely in Will's heart. 'I beg your pardon,' he said, with some discomposure. 'What do you mean?'

'Look at me, and you will find your eyesight swim. Raise your hand; it is dead-heavy. This is your last bottle of wine, Master Will, and your last night upon the earth.' 'You are a doctor?' quavered Will. 'The best that ever was,' replied the other; 'for I cure both mind and body with the same prescription. I take away all pain and I forgive all sins; and where my patients have gone wrong in life, I smooth out all complications and set them free again upon their feet.' 'I have no need of you,' said Will. 'A time comes for all men, Master Will,' replied the doctor, 'when the helm is taken out of their hands. For you, because you were prudent and quiet, it has been long of coming, and you have had long to discipline yourself for its reception. You have seen what is to be seen about your mill; you have sat close all your days like a hare in its form: but now that is at an end; and,' added the doctor, getting on his feet, 'you must arise and come with me.' 'You are a strange physician,' said Will, looking steadfastly upon his guest. 'I am a natural law,' he replied, 'and people call me Death.'

"'Why did you not tell me so at first?' cried Will, 'I have been waiting for you these many years. Give me your arm, and welcome.' 'Lean upon my arm,' said the stranger, 'for already your strength abates. Lean on me heavily as you need; for, though I am old, I am very strong. It is but three steps to my carriage, and there all your trouble ends. Why, Will,' he added, 'I have been yearning for you as if you were my own son; and of all the men that ever I came for in my long days, I have come to you most gladly. I am caustic, and sometimes offend people at first sight; but I am a good friend at heart to such as you.' 'Since Marjory was taken,' returned Will, 'I declare before God you were the only friend I had to look for.' So the pair went arm in arm across the courtyard.

"One of the servants awoke about this time, and heard the noise of horses pawing before he dropped asleep again; all down the valley that night there was a rushing as of a smooth and steady wind descending toward the plain; and when the world rose next morning, sure enough, Will o' the Mill had gone at last upon his travels."

Expositive Discourse deals with the statement of a theme in a logical manner, independent of its time or space relations.

"Exposition" means: "The act of exposing, laying open or bare, or displaying to public view; an explanation or interpretation; the act of expounding or setting out the meaning." Hyslop says: "Exposition is a process that deals largely, if not wholly, with abstract and general conceptions, while pure Description and Narration will be occupied with concrete things, and will consider individual objects and their qualities without distinction between the essential and the accidental. But Exposition when dealing with the thought wholes must limit its process to the essential properties or events brought together."

Hill says: "Exposition may be briefly defined as *explanation*. It does not address the imagination, the feelings, or the will. It addresses the understanding exclusively, and it may deal with any subject-matter with which the understanding has to do. In the fact that Exposition does not appeal to the emotions lies the essential difference between Exposition and Description or Narration. Theoretically, Exposition treats the matter in hand with absolute impartiality, setting forth *the pure truth*,—the truth unalloyed by prejudice, pride of opinion, exaggeration of rhetoric, or glamour of sentiment. Except in works of a technical character, Exposition in this strict sense is comparatively rare."

While Description and Narrative are concerned with the statement of things or events, Exposition is limited to *abstract subjects* or *general ideas*, as for example: Truth; Time; Space; Beauty; Science; Philosophy; Religion; or Man (in the abstract); the Renaissance; the New Thought; Courage, etc. A true Definition is an Exposition. A scientific description is often really an Exposition, as for example Prof. Lodge's lectures on "The Ether of Space." A consideration of the abstract qualities of a concrete thing is also an Exposition. The prime requisite of a good Exposition is *clearness*, and clearness is gained only by logical and orderly arrangement. As an authority has said: "Good arrangement is at least one-half of sound exposition. Order is often equivalent to explanation." The authorities agree that the best arrangement consists in beginning with the simpler phases of the subject—the features best understood by the hearer—and then gradually proceeding, by logical steps, to the more complex and less understood phases or features.

The following quotation from Clodd's "Story of Creation" will serve as an example of a short but clear Expositive Discourse:

"MATTER.—Under this term are comprised all substances that occupy space and affect the senses. Matter is manifest in four states—solid, liquid, gaseous, and ultra-gaseous in the form of electrically-charged corpuscles projected into space. It is probably also present throughout the universe in the highly tenuous form called ether. Between the above states there is no absolute break, matter assuming any one of them according to the relative strength of the forces which bind, and of the energies which loosen, the component parts of bodies; in other words, according to the temperature or pressure. *E. g.,* water becomes solid when its latent heat or contained motion is dissipated, and gaseous to invisibility when its particles are driven asunder by heat. Since the ultimate nature of matter remains unknown and unknowable, we can only infer what it *is* by learning what it *does.* The actions of bodies, whatever their states, are explicable only on the assumption that the bodies are made up of infinitely small particles which, in their combined state as mechanical units, are called molecules; and in their free state, as chemical units, are called atoms. The molecule is a combined body reduced to a limit that cannot be passed without altering its nature. The atoms, or so-called elementary substances, number, as far as is known at present, between seventy and eighty, but many of them are extremely rare, and exist in such minute quantities as to be familiar only to the chemist. They were called 'atoms' on the assumption of their indivisibility, but this has been recently disproved. The atom is an aggregation of what are called 'electrons,' which are in 'a state of rapid interlocked motion,' and concerning which, Sir Oliver Lodge says, 'It is a fascinating guess that they contain the fundamental substratum of which all matter is composed. * * * On this view, the ingredient of which the whole of matter is made up, is nothing more or less than electricity.' It is estimated that an atom of hydrogen contains 700 electrons; an atom of sodium 16,000, and an atom of radium 160,000. An atom of matter possessing an electron in excess is called an 'ion,' and it is the 'ions' which act, a negative charge causing the impulse to motions of enormous velocity. Each atom may be compared with the solar or stellar systems as containing a number of bodies moving In rapid orbits. But the comparison falls when the age of the one and that of the other is estimated, since 'it is probable that the changes in the foundation stones of the universe, the more stable elemental atoms themselves, must require a period to be expressed only by millions of millions of centuries." Although no known energy that we can apply can separate any one atom into two, so that, as Dalton said, 'no man can spilt an atom,' we do not any longer speak of atoms in the words of Clerk Maxwell, as 'the foundation stones of the material universe, unchanged and unchangeable, not capable of wear, but as true to-day as when they were coined at the mint of the mighty Artificer.' Nothing escapes the law of change. The shrewd speculations of Heraclitus the Ionian, who lived two thousand five hundred years ago, that everything is in a state of flux, and, therefore, that the universe is always 'becoming,' have added confirmation in every discovery of modern physics. An atom, say, of oxygen, entering into myriad combinations, may exhibit the same qualities for millions upon millions of years, but its destiny to ultimately become something other than it is, perchance every atom dissolved, as Sir William Crookes suggests, into 'the formless mist' of protyle—assumed the primordial matter—is irrevocable."

But it must not be supposed that Expositive Discourse is intended only for the purpose of technical or scientific explanation. The lawyer uses it in expounding the principles of the law involved, and the rules of evidence in question; the physician when he is discussing the nature of some particular form of disease; the professor when he is teaching his particular branch; the literary or dramatic critic when he is discussing the merits of a book or play; and the financier when he is setting forth the general features of investment or finance. In Exposition, both Description and Narration are frequently included, in order to illustrate and explain certain points and features of the general subject. And Exposition often invades the province of Argument, when it goes beyond the *pure explanation* of the general subject, and seeks to urge the merits of some particular theory involved. The various forms of Discoursive Expression are not to be separated from each other, and placed in different mental compartments—on the contrary, they shade and blend into each other, forming many interesting combinations. The classification is adopted principally for convenience in analysis and study of the principles involved.

CHAPTER X.

ARGUMENTATIVE DISCOURSE

A RGUMENTATIVE DISCOURSE deals with the process of convincing or persuading of the understanding, by proofs or presentation of evidence, to the end that the opinion or will, or both, of the hearer may be influenced. "Argument," in its popular usage, means: "The act or process of reasoning, contention, controversy; that about which arguing, debate, or reasoning takes place, or the reasons adduced; the reasons adduced in support of any assertion."

In its technical usage in Logic, it is defined and explained by Whately as follows: "An expression in which, from something laid down as granted, something else is deduced, *i. e.*, must be admitted to be true as necessarily resulting from the other. Thus, reasoning expressed in words is argument, and an argument stated at full length is a syllogism. Every argument consists of two parts—that which is proved, and that by which it is proved. Before the former is established it is called 'the question,' and when established, the 'conclusion' or 'inference,' and that which is employed to effect this result, the 'premises.'"

Watts says: "Argumentation is that operation of the mind whereby we infer one proposition from two or more propositions premised; or it is the drawing a conclusion, which before was unknown or doubtful, from some propositions more known and evident." Another authority says: "Argumentation is the act or process of reasoning; that is, of drawing a deductive inference from premises given, or of inductively making a generalization from a multitude of facts carefully brought together and sifted."

Hill says: "Argument, like exposition, addresses the understanding, but there is an important difference between the two. Exposition achieves its purpose if it makes the persons addressed *understand* what is said; argument achieves its purpose if it makes them *believe* that what is maintained *is true*; exposition aims at *explaining*, argument at *convincing*. The difference between an argument and an exposition may be shown by a comparison between the address of an advocate to the jury, and the charge of the judge. The advocate tries to convince the jury that his client has the right on his side; the judge, if he has the truly judicial spirit, tries to make the jury understand the question at issue exactly as it is."

As we have said in the preceding chapter, Exposition often invades the field of argument, and skilfully brings into relief certain sides of the general question, or else emphasizes certain aspects of the case, so that the *explanation* is transformed into an *argument*. And, likewise, Argument may clothe itself in the garb of Exposition, so that while to ordinary outward appearance it is merely an *explanation*, the effect of that explanation is really one of the most effective forms of argument. Moreover, in every lengthy argument, there must of necessity be more or less Exposition, or explanation of that which is to be proved. And, likewise, the majority of Arguments are preceded by Exposition, or explanation of that upon which the Argument is to be based.

Hyslop says: "Description, Explanation, and Exposition are processes by which we endeavor to narrate facts and thoughts in a systematic and orderly manner. They are designed to give an intelligible and methodical conception of the data that are connected with a particular theme. But they are not designed to convince the mind. They may incidentally do this, but it is not the primary object to create conviction. They are occupied with the formation and presentation of clear conceptions, systematic and methodical discourse, which does as much to make ideas intelligible as it does to please the sense of order. But Proof and Argumentation go beyond this. They endeavor to remove doubt, to give belief and knowledge to the intellect."

The ancients, who placed the highest value upon Argumentative Discourse, particularly in the form of orations, and who reduced this form of expression to a fine art and almost to an exact science, divided the Formal Argument into six steps, as follows: (1) The Exordium or Introduction; (2) the Division; (3) the Statement; (4) the Reasoning; (5) the Appeal to the Emotions; and (6) the Peroration or Closing.

Modern authorities incline to the opinion that this arrangement is rather too artificial for effectiveness and easy expression, and the employment of it to-day is apt to produce the effect of pedantry or stiffness. But, a close analysis will show that these successive steps, or at least some of them, are employed to-day in every argument, long or short, from the address of the lawyer, or the sermon of the preacher, to the "selling talk" of the modern salesman. Whether or not this be recognized, it will be well for the student to consider these several steps of the ancients, in order that he may grasp the meaning of each and thus be able to employ any or all of them when occasion necessitates it. Accordingly, we shall follow this arrangement in considering the Principles of Argument.

The Exordium or Introduction of an Argument is generally conceded to be one of its most difficult steps. It is important that the person making the argument make a good impression upon his hearers so as to render them attentive, well-disposed, and open to persuasion as he proceeds. The following suggestions, representing the opinion of some of the best authorities, are offered regarding the Introduction:

I. Endeavor to create the impression of earnestness, dignity and self-respect. There is nothing so impressive or contagious as earnestness, and nothing so hurtful as an apparent lack of it. The speaker who can make his hearers feel at the start that he believes in what he is saying—in the cause he is about to undertake, has scored heavily at the beginning, and has paved the road to a successful progress in his argument. On the other hand, he who causes his hearers to doubt his earnestness, or his belief in the justice and strength of his cause, is handicapped from the beginning. But one should not commit the mistake of *telling* his hearers *in words* that he believes in his cause—he should convey the impression by the suggestion of his manner and mental attitude. The conviction and earnestness of a speaker need not be told in words to his hearers, any more than the virtue of a woman or the honesty of a man need be verbally asserted to those to whom they come in contact—they must be suggested to others by one's acts and manner. The man who cries: "I am honest;" the woman who continually asserts, "I am virtuous;" or the speaker who tells his hearers, "I am in earnest," himself raises the question and is in danger of being misunderstood and doubted. Some things must be left to the power of suggestion. Dignity and self-respect are qualities which favorably impress hearers, and the lack of them tend to lessen one's influence. But, remember that dignity does not mean *pomposity*; nor does *self-respect* mean manifest *egotism or foolish pride!*

II. Endeavor to attract the Attention of your hearers at the start. Attention is the first step in any mental process, and he who would persuade or convince his hearers must first manage to secure their attention. Attention may be secured by presenting the opening features of the subject in a novel, attractive manner. The unusual always attracts the attention. If the curiosity of the hearers can be aroused, attention results naturally. Attention depends largely upon interest. Interest may be aroused by presenting the subject in a novel, *new* manner, and may be held by changing the object or subject presented to it. Interest grows tired when the subject grows monotonous—

it demands variety. It will be well to observe the following two rules of Attention and Interest, as given by Halleck: "(1) Attention will not attach itself firmly to uninteresting things; (2) It will soon decline in vigor, (a) if the stimulus is unvarying, or (b) if some new attribute is not discovered in the object."

III. Let your Introduction appear easy and natural, rather than labored or stilted. The conversational tone is effective, and tends to establish a feeling of intimacy between speaker and hearers. Cicero says that "The Introduction must appear to have sprung up of its own accord from the matter under consideration." He held that in preparing an address or speech, the Introduction should not be composed until the later steps of the discourse have been completed, or at least until the succeeding steps of the argument are fully planned out and digested. In this way, he held, the Introduction will be full and complete, and in perfect harmony with the thought and words to follow it. This advice is approved by some of the best later authorities.

IV. While you should arouse interest and curiosity by your Introduction, you should avoid claiming too much at this stage, or promising too much. It is well to exercise a little modesty here, for if you create expectations which you cannot realize, or make statements which you afterward fail to "make good" you create a feeling of disappointment, doubt and impression of failure. It is well to be bold and positive in your opening claims, but this is far different from making claims which cannot be substantiated. Better a "measure heaped full and running over" of fulfilment, than "a sky-rocket introduction and a falling-stick finish."

V. Avoid passionate appeal, vehemence, or strong feeling in the beginning. It is far better to appear to be laboring under repressed feeling and emotion, than to burst into feeling at the start. Save your emotion and feeling for later steps. The minds of your hearers should be led step by step toward strong feeling or passionate appeal. If, however, the nature of the subject is one allied to passionate feeling, the latter may be subtly *suggested* in the beginning, and then apparently held back for the appeal to reason.

VI. Never anticipate a material argument, or effective point of your argument, in your Introduction. You waste your powder by failing to observe this precept. Confine yourself to general statements in your opening, and save your heavy ammunition until the stage in which it will count.

VII. Measure your Introduction by your main discourse. Do not preface a short, argumentative discourse by a long Introduction, nor a long discourse by a trifling Introduction. As an authority has said: "The Introduction should be accommodated, both in length and character, to the discourse that is to follow; in length, as nothing can be more absurd than to erect an immense vestibule before a diminutive building; and in character, as it is no less absurd to overcharge with superb ornaments the portico of a plain dwelling-house, or to make the entrance to a monument as gay as that to an arbor."

The Division of an Argument is that step in the discourse in which the speaker states the general method or plan of argument to be followed, and the heads or divisions of the subject of the discourse. This step of the Argument is often omitted, particularly in cases in which the nature of the argument confines it to one or more leading points. Some of the best authorities advise speakers to omit this step of argument wherever possible, citing the tiresome and tedius practice of the old-time preacher with his interminable "heads" and "divisions"—his "thirdly" and "fourthly"—as a horrible example. But even if this step be omitted, the speaker should observe a formal plan of division and method in his address.

Quackenbos says: "A formal Division is used more frequently in the sermon than in any other species of composition; but it has been questioned by many whether the laying down of heads, as it is called, does not lessen, rather than add to, the effect. The Archbishop of Cambray, in his Dialogues on Eloquence, strongly condemns it, observing that it is a modern invention, which took its rise only when metaphysics began to be introduced into preaching; that it renders a sermon stiff and destroys its unity; and is fatal to oratorical effect. It is urged on the other hand, however, that a formal division renders a sermon more clear by showing how all the parts hang on each other and tend to one and the same point, and thus makes it more impressive and instructive. The heads of a sermon, moreover, are of great assistance to the memory of the hearer; they enable him to keep pace with the progress of the discourse, and afford him resting places whence he can reflect on what has been said, and look forward to what is to follow."

The best of the modern authorities seem to incline to the opinion that *instead of employing a formal statement of the Division to be followed in the discourse, the speaker would better suggest the division and heads of his discourse in his Statement,* not technically or formally, but incidentally—the suggestion being expressed by the order observed in the various points in the Statement. But this does not relieve the speaker from observing the rules of the Division in preparing his discourse, making his notes (if he uses this method), and of mentally arranging and classifying his subject. The following rules are approved by some of the best authorities:

I. Let the division between the various parts or sub-divisions be *distinct*—avoid the common error of including one sub-division in another.

II. Let the division be natural, and along the natural "lines of cleavage" or separation, rather than artificial classification.

III. Let each division or sub-division include and exhaust its entire subject-matter. Leave no "loose ends" or "unclassified residuum."

IV. Let your divisions and sub-divisions be sufficiently general and large to avoid a tedious and unnecessary multiplication of heads.

V. Let the division follow the arrangement of *first the simplest points*, and then the more difficult ons arising from the former—always rising from the simple toward the complex or difficult.

Other rules bearing upon the question of Division will appear in connection with the subject of the Statement, which follows.

The Statement of an Argument is that step in the discourse in which the general and leading facts of the subject of discourse are presented briefly for the consideration of the hearer. There is quite a difference between the various authorities regarding the value of, and most effective method of presenting, the Statement. Some hold that the Statement should form a part of the Introduction, if not indeed superseding the latter; while others incline to the idea herein favored, i e., that it is advisable to first attract the attention of the hearers by a short Introduction, before proceeding to a formal presentation of the Statement.

Sheppard says: "It is unwise to weary the imagination of the hearer, because you are sure by that means to weary his muscles and sinews. It will weary his imagination to be told at the start what you propose to accomplish before you stop. It will weary him to tell him that after you have done so and so you will do so and so, and then so and so, and finally and in conclusion, so and so. Go on and do it. Say your say and be done with it. Never say: 'Before I pass to the preliminary remarks, by way of preface to the introduction to the first head of my sixteen heads, I wish to remark, in the first place, that—but, by the way, before I pass to that, I wish to say that, etc.'" The same writer quotes approvingly the criticism that the late Moses Stuart preached a sermon in which he (1) "occupied a large part of an hour telling his audience what he was not going to preach about, of errors he was not going to combat; giving (2) a sketch of the heresies alluded to; (3) a few strokes designed to show how easily they could be demolished if he should take the time, and (4) the real instruction for unlearned hearers who cared nothing for exploded theories, was summed up in a few paragraphs."

Hill says, in answer to the question, "Should the proposition or the proof come first!" "* * * If the proposition is familiar to the persons addressed, there will usually be some advantage in beginning with what is novel in the proof; for an old conclusion acquires fresh interest when regarded from a new point of view or approached by a new path. If the proposition, whether familiar or not to the persons addressed, is likely to awaken hostility, it should not be announced until steps have been taken to procure for it a favorable reception. Often the best course to this end is to begin by stating the question at issue without indicating the desired conclusion until some of the arguments on each side have been presented; or it may be wise to begin by securing assent to general principles from which the desired conclusion can be logically deduced. In pursuing either course, a reasoner seems to invite his readers or hearers to join him in an inquiry for the truth. This inquiry results, if he is successful, in convincing them of the justness of his conclusion by leading them to convince themselves; it results, if he is unsuccessful, in inducing them to give attention to evidence to which they would have turned a deaf ear had they known to what conclusion it led. In the absence of such considerations as these, *the better course usually is first to state what is to be proved, and then to prove it!*

The following general rules regarding the Statement are approved of by good authorities:

I. State your proposition in a clear, forcible and brief style. Clear, that the points may be easily understood; Forcible, that they make an impression on the minds of your hearers; Brief, that they may be easily remembered.

II. Adhere to *the true facts of the case*, and yet endeavor to emphasize and fix the attention of your hearers upon the features and points which are favorable to your contention, while keeping in the shadow of the attention those which are opposed thereto. Turn the "spotlight" upon your strong

Points—this will not only illuminate them, but will tend to throw in the background the opposing ones.

III. If the proposition is complex or intricate, it will be well to avail yourself of the rules for Division, to some extent, and to briefly, concisely, and clearly analyze and divide the proposition in accordance therewith. In this case, care should be taken to follow the same arrangement, division and order in the succeeding steps of the argument, as otherwise there is a tendency to confuse the minds of your hearers.

IV. Adhere to the arrangement, division and grouping indicated by your Statement, when you come to the steps of Proof, Persuasion, or Appeal to Emotion. Many an otherwise good speaker impairs the efficiency of his work by making a logical statement of his argument, and then apparently ignoring it in his subsequent discourse. This practice, or malpractice, is akin to announcing a discourse on a certain subject, and then substituting another on an entirely different subject.

V. Let the statement of points of easy proof precede that of points more difficult. Let the statement of simple points precede that of more complex points.

VI. Regarding the statement of forthcoming arguments, observe the following arrangement: (1) Arguments of Cause and Effect; (2) Arguments of Analogy; (3) Arguments of Association. (See next chapter for this classification.) Some authorities vary the statement of this rule in favor of the following: (1) Causes; (2) Examples and Instances; (3) Indications and Signs. Remember that the form of the Statement must be followed in the course of the argument.

VII. Avoid the tendency and temptation to inject Argumentative Proof into your Statement. Reserve your artillery fire until the psychological moment. The statement is merely the "promise of proofs to come."

Lord Abinger, an eminent advocate, said: "I found from experience, as well as theory: that the most essential part of speaking is to make yourself understood. For this purpose it is absolutely necessary that the Court and jury should know as early as possible *de qua re agitur*. It was my habit, therefore, to state in the simplest form that the truth and the case would admit the proposition of which I maintained the affirmative and the defendant's counsel the negative."

CHAPTER XI

ARGUMENTATION

THE FOURTH step in an Argument is that of *Reasoning*, which is the great step or phase, and to or from which all else leads or follows. Reasoning is the *essence* of the Argument. This step of the Argument may be divided into two stages, i. e., (1) The Proposition or statement of that which is to be proved or disproved; and (2) The Proof or Discourse in which is embodied all that tends to prove or disprove the Proposition. The purpose of the Argument is to convince and persuade the hearers that the proof adduced is sufficient to sustain or refute the proposition.

The Proposition is usually introduced in the Statement. It is of the utmost importance that one should thoroughly understand and explain to his hearers the exact thing that he undertakes to prove or disprove. The issue should be made perfectly plain and clear. As Hill well says: "Nothing can free a writer or a speaker from the obligation of having the proposition distinctly fixed in his own mind before he begins his argument; for he cannot safely take the first step toward proving a proposition until he knows exactly what proposition is to be proved. The process of investigation, by which a man arrives at certain conclusions, should be completed before the argumentative process, by which he endeavors to convince others of the correctness of those conclusions, can advantageously be begun." We have seen, in the consideration of the Statement, the necessity of making clear to one's hearers the real point or points at issue. The issue, or true point of dispute and argument, should be discovered and clearly stated before the argument proceeds to the stage of proof or disproof.

Hyslop says of Probation or Proof: "Probation is the process of proof, the statement and arrangement of facts and truths which will establish belief or knowledge in regard to the proposition at issue, or the contrary. The thesis or issue is the proposition to be proved or disproved. The truths which prove or disprove it are the known facts and principles which may constitute the premises, and the thesis will be the conclusion. These determining truths may be axioms, postulates, proved propositions, or any truth or fact which the person to whom the probation is presented may accept. Their acceptance is the condition of their proving or disproving anything. We must observe, therefore, that probation, as here discussed, is a material as well as a formal process. The object in proof is not merely to have correct reasoning, but also to have correct and true propositions. We must, therefore, enunciate some facts or principles accepted by the person to whom the probation is presented, and then bring the thesis or issue under it in such a way as to enforce conviction, or at least make it the most probable alternative. * * * Whenever any proposition is asserted or made the subject of argument, the object is to show whether it be true or false. The general method of argumentation is the same for both sides. *But the proposition at the outset is supposed not to represent any conviction in favor of or against itself*, but to be balanced between belief and disbelief, or certitude and denial. The problem is to influence the judgment so that it will decide in favor of or against the proposition. Proof or confirmation is the process of determining the conviction one way or the other, and of removing the balance or doubt so that some degree of assent or denial, whether of belief or knowledge, will follow as a consequence."

The authorities first divide Proof into two general classes; viz., (1) Direct Proof, or the process of sustaining a given proposition; and (2) Indirect Proof, or the process of refuting objections to a given proposition. Of course, the refuting of an objection to a given proposition does not directly *prove* the proposition itself, but it removes from the argument an obstacle to direct proof and is therefore of value, indirectly.

Another division of Proof is that of: (1) Proof by Deductive Argumentation; and (2) Proof by Inductive Argumentation. Proof by Deductive Argumentation is that in which Deductive Reasoning is employed—where the process of reasoning seeks to derive a particular truth from a general truth. Thus, from the general truth that "All men are mortal," and the fact that "Socrates is a *man*," we may prove by Deductive Argumentation that "Socrates is mortal." Proof by Inductive Argumentation is that in which Inductive Reasoning is employed—where the process of reasoning seeks to derive a general truth from particular truths. Thus, from the particular truths that "Heat will expand iron, zinc, copper, gold, silver, etc." we may prove by Inductive Argumentation that "Heat will expand *all* metals."

Of course, all general truths must have been originally reasoned by induction from particular truths, and being so established have become bases for deductive reasoning from which particular truths may be established. There are certain general truths or principles which are generally accepted as *axiomic* or "self-evident truth," without the necessity of argument. In Deductive Argumentation, the argument proceeds from an accepted general truth and attempts to establish the fact that a particular proposition comes under, or is included in, that general truth, and is thus a particular truth. In Inductive Argumentation, the argument proceeds to show the apparent existence of a general truth in a number of particular things, from which it may be supposed or reasonably believed that the general law exists as a truth. The rule in Inductive Reasoning is that: "The probability of a hypothesis is in proportion to the number of facts and phenomena it will explain."

Arguments may be classified, according to form, as follows: (1) Argument based upon Cause and Effect; (2) Argument based upon Analogy; (3) Argument based upon Association.

Argument based upon Cause and Effect is sometimes known as "Argument from Antecedent Probability." It is based upon the general principle or axiom that: "From the same causes, under the same circumstances, the same results will flow." This axiom is based upon man's belief in the uniformity of natural laws. From this, we arrive at the belief that given a certain cause, under certain circumstances, we may safely infer the presence of a certain effect; or given a certain effect, under certain circumstances, we may safely infer the presence of a certain cause. In order to reason or argue along these lines, however, we must understand that there are certain "Tests of Casual Agency" accepted by logicians, by which we may ascertain the casual agency in any particular case, and thus make an inductive inference. These "tests" are as follows:

I. *The Method of Agreement*: "If, whenever a given object or agency is present, without counteracting forces, a given effect is produced, there is strong evidence that the object or agency is the cause of the effect."

II. *The Method of Difference*: "If, when the supposed cause is present the effect is present, and when the supposed cause is absent the effect is wanting, there being in neither case any other agents present to effect the result, we may reasonably infer that the supposed cause is the real one."

III. *The Method of Residues*: "When in any phenomena we find a result remaining after the effects of all known causes are estimated, we may attribute it to a residual agent not yet reckoned."

IV. *The Method of Concomitant Variations*: "When a variation in a given antecedent is accompanied by a variation of a given consequent, they are in some manner related as cause and effect."

Atwater says of the above: "When either of these criteria is found, free from conflicting evidence, and especially when several of them concur, the evidence is clear that the cases observed are fair representatives of the whole class, and warrant a valid universal inductive conclusion."

Argument based upon Cause and Effect may be employed in arguing the probability of the occurrence of a certain effect arising from an admitted cause; or in arguing the probability of the occurrence of a certain effect arising from an admitted cause; or in arguing the probability of the existence of a certain precedent cause by reason of a certain cause to effect; the other from effect to cause. Thus we may argue that from the admitted existence of certain casual agencies, belonging to a class of causes which have resulted in certain effect in the past, there will arise certain effects in the future. As for example, we may argue that as John Smith is drinking to excess, and that this cause has resulted in drunkenness and poverty in other cases in the past, therefore, John Smith is likely to become a drunkard and a pauper in the future. Or, that undue familiarity existing in a certain case, and familiarity having been known to "breed contempt" in the past, therefore, contempt is apt to arise from the present manifestation of familiarity. Likewise, we may argue that from the existence of certain admitted effects, there must have existed a certain precedent cause. Thus, we may argue that there being an egg before us, and from the fact that eggs have always been known to have been laid by birds or fowls, therefore, the present egg must have been laid by a bird or fowl. Or, that a coin having disappeared from a drawer, and persons having been known to steal coins in the past, therefore, some person must have stolen the coin. The doctrine of Causation, or the theory that nothing exists with a cause, and that everything proceeds from a precedent cause, and must, in itself, be the cause of a subsequent effect, is well grounded in human reason and experience, and argument based thereon is of the strongest character. The question of "motive" belongs to this form of argument.

Argument based upon Analogy is sometimes known as "Argument from Resemblance," or "Argument from Example." It is based upon the general principle or axiom that: "*If two or more things resemble each other in many points, they will probably resemble each other in many other points.*" The principle involved in this form of Argument may be gathered from the following quotations from two well-known authorities:

Jevons says: "If I see a machine with boiler, cylinder, air-pump, piston-rod, crank, and other parts exactly resembling those of a steam-engine, I do not hesitate to call it a steam-engine, to assert that it has a piston, valves, and other hidden parts, like all steam engines. It is in the same way that we reason about the substance of which anything is made. If a person offers me a shilling as change, how can I be sure that it is a good shilling, and made of silver? All that I can do is to examine the coin, and observe whether it has a fine pure white lustre where the surface is rubbed; whether there is in other parts of the surface the black tarnish peculiar to silver; whether the coin seems to be hard, and gives a sharp ringing sound when thrown down. If it has all these characters and, moreover, has a good impression exactly like that seen on other shillings issued from the mint, then it is doubtless made of silver, and is a true shilling, that is to say, it will show all the other properties of standard silver, when examined in a manner suited for showing them."

Reid says: "We may observe a very great similitude between this earth which we inherit, and the other planets, Saturn, Jupiter, Mars, Venus and Mercury. They all revolve around the sun, as the earth does, although at different distances and in different periods. They borrow all their light from the sun, as the earth does. Several of them are known to revolve around their axis like the earth, and by that means have like succession of day and night. Some of them have moons, that serve to give them light in the absence of the sun, as our moon does to us. They are all, in their motions, subject to the same law of gravitation as the earth is. From all this similitude it is not unreasonable to think that these planets may, like our earth, be the habitation of various orders of living creatures. There is some probability in this conclusion from analogy."

Argument based upon Analogy is quite popular, and in many cases it is valid. From the very nature of things we are compelled to resort to this form of reasoning and expression in the absence of the direct proof of positive evidences of the senses covering the entire proposition or points at issue. As Brooks says: "This principle is in constant application in ordinary life and in science. A physician visiting a patient, says this disease corresponds in several particulars with typhoid fever, hence it will correspond in all particulars, and *is* typhoid fever. So, when a geologist discovers a fossil animal with large, strong, blunt claws, he infers that it procured its food by scratching or burrowing in the earth. It was by analogy that Dr. Buckland constructed an animal from a few fossil bones, and, when subsequently the bones of the entire animal were discovered, his construction was found to be correct."

But there is a limit to reasoning by Analogy, and the argument based thereon. There is a great danger of falling into the fallacies connected with this form of reasoning—and, in fact, many speakers deliberately advance these fallacies hoping thereby to deceive and delude their hearers. Jevons says: "Reasoning by analogy is found to be a very uncertain guide. In some cases unfortunate mistakes are committed. Children are sometimes killed by gathering and eating poisonous berries, wrongly inferring that they can be eaten, because other berries, of a somewhat similar appearance, have been found agreeable and harmless. Poisonous toadstools are occasionally mistaken for mushrooms, especially by persons not accustomed to gather them. * * * The beaten dog fears every stick, and there are few dogs which will not run away when you pretend to pick up a stone, even though there be no stone to pick up."

Brooks says: "The argument from Analogy is plausible, but often deceptive. Thus to infer that since American swans are white the Australian swan is white, gives a false conclusion, for it is really black. So to infer that because John Smith has a red nose, and is a drunkard, that Henry Jones who has also a red nose is also a drunkard, would be a dangerous inference. * * * Conclusions of this kind, drawn from analogy, are frequently fallacious. Mandeville uses the following argument against popular education: 'If the horse knew enough, he would soon throw his rider.' He intends to imply two pairs of related terms; thus 'As the horse is to the rider, so are the people to their rulers;' which is, of course, a fallacy, since the relations are not similar."

Hill says: "* * * the danger lies in making a hasty generalization from insufficient data and ignoring whatever supports an opposite conclusion. This fallacy is committed by those who argue from the examples of Franklin and Lincoln that men who do not go to college are more likely to succeed in life than men who do, and by those who argue from a few instances of the use or non-use of tobacco, that marriage or celibacy conduces to a long life, that a quick temper goes with red hair, or good nature with blue eyes, that a college degree implies scholarship."

Jevons says: "There is no way in which we can really assure ourselves that we are arguing safely by analogy." Brooks says: "The probability of analogy depends upon the number of observed resemblances. Every similarity which is noticed between two objects increases the probability that the two objects resemble each other in some other property. * * * In comparing two objects, the differences as well as the similarities must be taken into consideration."

Many persons, untrained in logical thinking, ·often mistake figurative illustrations, metaphor, etc., for forms of analogous proof. Hill says: "One who perceives many analogies is in danger of mistaking fanciful for real ones, of making a mere metaphor do duty as an argument." Mill cites Bacon as being "equally conspicuous in the use and abuse of figurative illustration." "George Eliot says: "O Aristotle! if you had had the advantage of being "the freshest modern" instead of the greatest ancient, would you not have mingled your praise of metaphorical speech, as a sign of high intelligence, with a lamentation that intelligence so rarely shows itself in speech without metaphor— that we can so seldom declare what a thing is, except by saying it is something else!"

Argument based upon Association has for its general principle the well-known Law of the Association of Ideas and Things. This form of argument is closely allied to what is called Circumstantial Evidence. Hyslop says: "This is a form of inductive and synthetic proof, and is that form of argument which endeavors to prove a thesis by the presence of certain signs or incidents which suggest it. * * * A man is charged with murder. We wish to prove the accusation. We find certain characteristics in the boot tracks going away from the murdered person. If we find that the boots of the accused correspond exactly to these characteristics, we have at least presumptive evidence of his guilt. If, further, we find that the accused possesses bullets or slugs like those found in the body of the murdered person, we have corroborative circumstantial evidence. Unless this can be of a large and cumulative amount or of a particular quality, it does not suffice for demonstrative proof, but only establishes a certain degree of probability. It is simply an argument from certain signs, marks, characteristics, coincidences, etc., to the probability that a given thesis is true. Whenever we argue from any given attribute or phenomenon to an unknown cause, we in fact employ the argument from circumstantial evidence * * *"

Hill says: "The force of an argument from sign (association) depends, moreover, not upon the magnitude of that which serves as a sign, but also upon the closeness of its connection with the thing signified. It matters not how trifling a circumstance is in itself if it is a link in a chain of evidence. 'A skilful forgery is detected by an inspection of small points; a mutilated body has been identified by a peculiarity of the teeth; a murderer has been tracked by the print of the nails in his shoes."

This form of Argument is generally associated with a Hypothesis, the associated ideas and facts, and the circumstantial evidence, serving to support or sustain the hypothesis itself. A hypothesis is: "A supposition or conjecture to account for facts or phenomena." The probability of a hypothesis is determined by the number of facts and phenomena it will explain. The larger the number of facts and phenomena explained or accounted for by a hypothesis, the greater is held to be its degree of probability. Verification of a hypothesis is obtained by showing that it will account for all the facts and phenomena in question. Some authorities hold that more than this is required for verification, and that perfect verification exists not simply when the hypothesis will account for all the facts and phenomena, but when also there is no other possible hypothesis which will account for them. It has been often found that an entire structure of circumstantial evidence built up around a certain hypothesis will also answer to verify another, and a totally different hypothesis.

In all argument there exists what is known as the Burden of Proof, which is an obligation resting upon those stating the proposition or advancing the hypothesis. The rule in the case is expressed by the legal maxim: "He who affirms must prove." Stephen, a celebrated authority upon Evidence, says: "The burden of proof as to any particular fact lies on that person who wishes the Court to believe in its existence, unless it is provided by any law that the burden of proving the fact shall lie on any particular person." In common discussion, the burden of proof is also held to rest upon the one who wishes to introduce a new thing as a substitute for an established thing, or who wishes to introduce a change. What is called the Presumption usually abides with the side opposed to that upon which the Burden of Proof rests. The Burden of Proof is always a disadvantage, and the Presumption always an advantage, for obvious reasons.

CHAPTER XII.

EVIDENCE AND PROOF

*E*VIDENCE IS defined as "the material of proof." There is a distinction between Evidence in Law, and Evidence in Logic. The distinction is brought out in the following definitions of the two, taken from the "Encyclopædic Dictionary."

Evidence (in Law): "Proof, either written or unwritten, of allegations in issue between parties. The following are the leading rules of procedure: (1) The sole object and end of evidence being to ascertain the several disputed points or facts in issue, no irrelevant evidence should be admitted. (2) The point in issue is to be proved by the party who asserts the affirmative. (3) Heresay evidence is not admitted."

Evidence (in Logic): "That which makes truth evident, or renders it evident to the mind that it is truth. It is generally limited to the proof of propositions as distinguished from axioms or institutions. Evidence is of two kinds, demonstrative and probable. Demonstrative evidence is of such a character that no person of competent intellect can fail to see that the conclusion is necessarily involved in the premises. Mathematics rest upon demonstrative evidence. All the propositions of Euclid are simply deductions from the definitions, axioms being assumed and postulates granted. But in every matter involving the establishment of concrete fact bearing on human conduct, demonstrative evidence is not obtainable, and the mind must content itself with probable evidence. Even in mathematics the premises are not concrete facts, but abstract hypotheses. Probable evidence is as if one held a delicate balance in the hand, casting into one scale every atom of evidence making for a proposition, and into the other all that could be adduced against it. According as one or the other scale predominates the proposition is accepted or rejected. Probable evidence may be of all conceivable degrees, from the faintest presumption to almost perfect certainty."

Evidence, to be strictly *direct* must reach one through his own senses or consciousness. It follows, then, that there can be but very little direct evidence used in an ordinary argument, and that we must of necessity fall back upon *indirect* evidence, or the evidence of the sense or consciousness of other persons, reaching us in the form of testimony, either verbal, written, or traditional. And, in both direct and indirect evidence, as above defined, we must always make the clear distinction between evidence of *facts* and the evidence of opinion, inference, interpretation, or prejudice regarding the actual facts, existing in the mind of the person experiencing them.

Testimony is the statement of the experience of another than the hearer. It may be true or false; that is, it may be a true statement of experience, or an untruth having no basis in fact, or possibly a half-truth, or truth colored with untruth. The general presumption is that testimony is true, the presumption arising from the general belief that a man will state what is true rather than what is false, particularly in absence of motive to the contrary. The reputation of a witness for falsehood tends to weaken the belief in his testimony, while his reputation for truth is likely to strengthen the belief in his veracity. But it is always remembered that even a notorious liar will sometimes tell the truth; and that an ordinarily truthful man may occasionally tell an untruth. The judgment, powers of observation, and general intelligence of the witness are also factors in determining the probable accuracy of his testimony. The subject of the testimony also has a bearing in this matter, for one will be able to testify more accurately about a subject with which he is well acquainted, than would one unfamiliar with that particular subject. The possibility of mistake or error is also taken into consideration.

It is also generally conceded that the beliefs, preconceived opinions, trend of mind, and general prejudice for or against, of a witness is apt to sway his judgment and observation, usually unconsciously, and to influence his testimony to some extent. There are very few people who can rise above these influences in making observations or in relating experiences. We *generally see that for which we look*, and are apt to tell of things as we think they might have, or should have been, rather than as they actually were. The personal bias must always be taken into consideration. The correspondence of the fact testified to with the general laws of nature and ordinary actions of things and persons is a point in the favor of its testimony, and *vice versa*. For instance, one testifying that he had seen a man with two heads, or an elephant with wings, might expect to be doubted. Testimony, cropping out incidentally in the main story, is generally held more likely to be true than untrue, for the false witness generally confines his lies to the main points of his story. Silence regarding an important point is generally construed as indicating the non-existence of the occurrence or event in question, owing to the great probability that it would have been brought out in the testimony had it existed.

The truth of testimony is held to be corroborated by the concurrence of other witnesses in the main points, particularly if the stories vary in irrelevant minor details instead of suspiciously agreeing upon even the minor points not material to the issue. No two persons ever tell exactly the same story regarding the same event experienced by both. Each relates what he saw and felt, in the light of his previous training, experience, and trend of character.

Chief Justice Shaw makes the following interesting and instructive distinction between Direct and Circumstantial Evidence:

"Each of these modes of proof has its advantages and disadvantages; it is not easy to compare their relative value. The advantage of positive evidence is, that you have the direct testimony of a witness to the fact to be proved, who, if he speaks the truth, saw it done; and the only question is, whether he is entitled to belief! The disadvantage is that the witness may be false and corrupt, and the case may not afford the means of detecting his falsehood. But, in a case of circumstantial evidence where no witness can testify directly to the fact to be proved, you arrive at it by a series of other facts, which by experience we have found so associated with the fact in question, as in the relation of cause and effect, that they lead to a satisfactory and certain conclusion; as when footprints are discovered after a certain snow, it is certain that some animated being has passed over the snow since it fell; and, from the form and number of the foot-prints, it can be determined with equal certainty, whether it was a man, a bird, or a quadruped. Circumstantial evidence, therefore, is founded on experience and observed facts and coincidences, establishing a connection between the known and proved facts and the fact sought to be proved. The advantages are, that, as the evidence commonly comes from several witnesses and different sources, a chain of circumstances is less likely to be falsely prepared and arranged, and falsehood and perjury are more likely to be detected and fail of their purpose. The disadvantages are, that a jury has not only to weigh the evidence of facts, but to draw just conclusions from them; in doing which, they may be led by prejudice or partiality, or by want of due deliberation and sobriety of judgment, to make hasty and false deductions; a source of error not existing in the consideration of positive evidence."

It must be remembered that what has been said in this chapter about Testimony, refers not only to verbal testimony, but also to the testimony contained in books and other writings, and to the testimony of tradition. The same general principles apply to all forms of testimony.

Hyslop says of Argument upon Testimony: "This is a form of argument based upon the credibility of a witness to real or alleged facts. The facts are circumstantial evidence of the thesis, and the character of the witness is a measure of the weight attaching to his testimony on the facts. 'The degree of weight to be attributed to testimony is always to be estimated by this view of the nature of testimony—that it is a sign, implying the facts to which it testifies as more or less necessary conditions of its having been given. Whenever, therefore, occasions or motives exist in the case for giving the testimony other than the truth, the credibility of the witness will be so far impaired. We are thus to judge of the credibility of historians. The historian of a sect or of a party must be received as a credible witness only so far as it may appear that truth was the condition of his speaking as he does. All admissions against his own sect or party, unless made as baits or lures, will be received as honest testimony. If these qualifications are wanting, there is nothing on which testimony can rest.' But where honesty and candor, as well as good judgment, exist, the facts attested will have all the weight of these qualities, though this may not be so great as in the case that the facts are personally known by the disputants."

Testimony may be not only as regards *facts*, but also as regards opinion, in which latter instance the testimony is known as "expert evidence." Expert evidence is the testimony of persons presumed to be competent to exercise a higher perception, judgment and discrimination in the particular subject, than the ordinary individual, by reason of their special training, experience and judgment. As Hyslop well expresses it: "It means to accept the judgment of qualified men where common experience is not a guide."

Evidence is the raw material from which the finished product of argument is woven. The grade of the product—its degree of fineness—its texture and weave—its adequacy and fitness for its purpose—all these things depend upon the skill of the weaver. And, moreover, the very color of the woven material, depends upon the art, science and skill of the artisan handling the material from its crude state until it emerges a finished article offered to the consideration of the public. From the same material is produced the coarsest fabric and the finest weave—the crudest hue and the most beautiful tints.

CHAPTER XIII.

FALSE ARGUMENT

I N THE process of Argumentative Discourse there frequently is manifested what is called False Argument, or Argument based upon Fallacy.

Fallacy is: "An unsound argument or mode of arguing, which while appearing to be decisive of a question, is in reality not so; an argument or proposition apparently sound, but really fallacious; a fallacious statement or proposition, in which the error is not apparent, and which is therefore likely to deceive or mislead; sophistry." The word is derived from the Latin word *fallax*, meaning "deceitful." While the question of Fallacy properly belongs to the subject of Logic, still various forms of Fallacy make their appearance as False Argument and very properly form a part of the general subject of Argumentative Discourse.

As Jevons says: "In learning how to do right it is always desirable to be informed as to the ways in which we are likely to go wrong. In describing to a man the road which he should follow, we ought to tell him not only the turnings which he is to take, but also the turnings which he is to avoid. Similarly, it is a useful part of logic which teaches us the ways and turnings by which people most commonly go astray in reasoning." Likewise, it is proper to inform the student of Argumentative Discourse of the false arguments, frequently used by persons engaged in debate or discussion, that he may guard himself against them by knowing their nature and form.

Omitting the technical fallacies condemned by the logicians, let us consider the leading fallacies employed as False Argument:

I. *Arguing from a true collective to a false particular.* As, for instance, to argue that because the Jewish race, as a whole, is distinguished for its keen business perception, that a particular Jew must be a keen business man. The individual Jew may be a very poor business man. Likewise, as Jevons points out: "Ministers sitting in cabinet council will probably come to a wise conclusion concerning an important question; but it does not follow that any one of them would come to a wise decision." Likewise, while statistics show that the percentage of Quakers in prison is very small compared to the whole number of prisoners, still it does not necessarily follow that all Quakers are honest, or even that the Quakers are any more honest than an equal number of people of any one other religious denomination— there is a very small percentage of Quakers in a community. The use of proverbs often comes under this head, for proverbs are notoriously ambiguous, and while possibly true of the race as a whole are often false of any particular individual.

II. *Arguing from uncertain meaning of words or terms.* The authorities say "A word or term with two meanings is really two words or two terms." The following familiar false argument illustrates this point in a humorous way: "A cat must have three tails, because (1) *Any* cat has *one* tail more than *no* cat; (2) *No* cat has *two* tails; therefore, (3) *Any* cat has *three* tails, *because any cat has one tail more than no cat.*" In the same way may be argued the 'truthfulness of a man who makes the statement: "I am telling a lie." If he is *lying,* he is *telling the truth,* because he has said he was lying; if he is *telling the truth,* he is *lying,* because he has so asserted. The remedy for this form of false argument is *the proper understanding and definition of the words and terms* used in the premises of an argument.

III. *Arguing a false conclusion. This arises from introducing into the conclusion new matter, or matter not contained in the original premises.* For instance the fallacious argument: (1) All men are mortal; (2) Socrates is a man; therefore (3) Socrates is wise. Or, De Morgan's celebrated illustration: "(1) Episcopacy is of Scripture origin; (2) The Church of England is the only Episcopal church in England; therefore, (3) The church established is the church that ought to be supported." Or as Jevons says: "The device of the Irishman who was charged with theft on the evidence of three witnesses who had seen him do it; he proposed to call thirty witnesses who had *not* seen him do it. Equally logical was the defense of the man who was called a materialist, and who replied, 'I am not a *materialist*; I am a *barber*.'"

IV. *Arguing a false cause.* Hyslop says: "It consists in arguing from a mere co-existence or sequence, a causal or necessary connection." It also often arises from a confusion of cause and effect, the latter being mistaken for the former. The old saying was: *after* a fact, therefore *because* of it." Thus the argument that as a pestilence arose *after* the appearance of a comet, the latter *caused* the former. Or, that a death of a king *following* the eclipse of the sun, was therefore *caused* by the latter. Or, that because cock-crowing is always heard *just before* the sunrise, therefore cock-crowing is the *cause* of the sunrise. Or, that because the greater the civilization, the greater the number of high silk hats, therefore high silk hats are the *cause* of civilization. Or, that because a certain Presidential candidate has been elected, the crops failed. A proper understanding of the rules of Cause and Effect will give one the antidote to this form of false reasoning.

V. *Arguing the ignorance of the opponent.* This form of false argument consists in claiming that a proposition is correct *because the opponent cannot prove the contrary.* This is in defiance of the rule regarding the Burden of Proof, and of the Presumption, as explained in a preceding chapter. It is the basest of all arguments, and yet is quite popular with some speakers. A moment's clear thought should serve to expose the fallacy. As Brooks says: "The fact that we cannot find a needle in the haystack is no proof that it is not there." A failure to prove an *alibi* is no proof of the guilt of a person accused of crime, but lawyers agree that nothing so prejudices a jury against a prisoner as the failure to sustain a claimed alibi. As Jevons well says: "No number of failures in attempting to prove a proposition really disprove it," and equally true is it that no number of failures to disprove a proposition really prove it. It is a favorite trick of some debaters to impudently claim: "I state that so-and-so is true, *and you cannot prove that it is not!*" This kind of argument would tend to prove that the moon was made of green cheese, simply *because no one could prove that it was not*. An understanding and application of the rules of Burden of Proof and of Presumption gives one the key to the situation.

VI. *Arguing beside the point*. This false argument consists in evading the point at issue. For instance, one asserts that A is *a thief*, and holds that he has established his proposition by evidence that A is a *liar*, and that as all thieves are liars, etc., in defiance of the fact that one may be a liar and yet not be a thief, and that, at any rate, A is accused of theft and not of lying. The writer has a personal recollection of a case in which a woman of the *demi monde* was accused of theft. No evidence whatsoever, direct or circumstantial, was adduced to show her connection with the alleged theft, but the prosecuting attorney tried to introduce extended evidence that the woman was a prostitute, and that as prostitutes often steal, the presumption was that she was a thief, etc. It is needless to say that the court ordered the discharge of the prisoner. We hear arguments of this kind in politics, as for instance, the argument that because a man was a good general, therefore he will make a good president. Or, that because a man is honest he will necessarily prove a good executive. To this class of false arguments belongs that cited by Hyslop as follows: "Church and State are good institutions; therefore, Church and State should be united." The false argument in this last case is in the assumption that because "Church and State are *good institutions*" may be proven, therefore is proven that "Church and State should be united." The real point to be proven, is either that "*All* good institutions should be united," or else the separate proof that "Church and State should be united."

VII. *Arguing in a Circle*. This form of false argument consists in "assuming as proof of a proposition, the proposition itself." For example the argument: (1) The Demopublican party is honest because it advocates honest principles; and (2) that certain principles are honest because they are advocated by the Demopublican party. Or that: (1) My church is the true church, because it was established by God; and (2) it must have been established by God, because it is the true church." Another instance is that of the quack physician who informs the father of a dumb girl of the cause of her trouble, as follows: "Nothing is more easy than to explain it, it comes from her having lost the power of speech." Or the explanation that "We can see through glass, because it is transparent." Or, "it is warm because it is summer; it is summer because it is warm." Hyslop says: "The fallacy of reasoning in a circle occurs mostly in long arguments where it can be committed without ready detection. In such cases as are given above, the fallacy is perfectly obvious. But where it occurs in a long discourse it may be committed without easy discovery. *It is likely to be occasioned by the use of synonyms which are taken to express more than the conception involved, when they really do not.*"

VIII. *Arguing by "Begging the Question."* This form of false argument consists in *the unwarranted assumption of the premise* upon which the argument is based. For instance, the example: "*Good institutions should be united*; Church and State are good institutions; therefore Church and State should be united." In this instance, the premise "Good institutions should be united" is *boldly assumed without proof or agreement.* Hyslop explains: "It is not merely the failure to prove one's premises that constitutes the fallacy of Begging the Question. The failure must be one which occurs when proof is needed or demanded, and this is when the premise in turn is treated as a conclusion to another argument. Hence the begging of the question occurs only when the attempt to prove a proposition involves the assumption of it in a premise that the hearer or opponent does not admit. * * * It is most frequent in arguments with others, because the one condition of proof or conviction in such cases is that the opponent, reader, or friend admit the principle upon which the conclusion is to be established, while the subject himself may not require proof at all for his conviction, as he already accepts the proposition. But we cannot prove to another a truth with premises that he does not admit. He simply charges 'begging the question' because he is not obliged to admit in the conclusion what he does not admit in the premises."

Arguing in a Circle is really one form of Begging the Question, although it differs in some respects from the more common forms of the latter. Begging the Question is a common practice of some debates, particularly in political discussions. Who has not known the orator, who solemnly and earnestly asserted: "It is a fact admitted by all, that," etc.; or "It is a truth disputed by none, that," etc.; or, "The wise of all ages and all lands, have held that," etc.; or, "The common experience of the race has demonstrated, beyond the possibility of doubt, that," etc.;—all of which is false argument, although the statement itself may be true—particularly aggravated instances of Begging the Question. There are also certain words and terms which have acquired a meaning, perhaps unwarranted, which prejudices one against anything to which they seem to be applicable, although there is no proof against the thing in question, nor even, in many cases, any proof that the quality indicated by the unpopular term is objectionable. Jevons calls these words and terms, "question-begging epithets," and says: "We should always be on our guard against being misled by them. It is a good proverb which says, 'Give a dog a bad name, and hang him.'"

IX. *Argument by Arousing Prejudice.* This form of false argument consists in an appeal to the passions and prejudices of the hearers, rather than to the intelligence and judgment. It is a favorite form of false argument in political addresses, and often in jury trials. It is the principal weapon of demagogues. Brooks says of it: "It does not *prove* anything, but may lead the judgment or actions of the people, and is therefore a fallacy. Such an argument is not improper when the conclusion arrived at is believed to be a correct one; but is illegitimate when the conclusion is wrong in itself, or when he who urges it does so hypocritically. Considered as an argument, it is always a fallacy, and should be used with great care and an upright conscience." Marc Antony's address over the body of Cæsar, as given by Shakespeare, is an excellent example of this form of false argument."

X. *Argument of Abuse.* This form of false argument is based on abuse of the opposing speaker, or browbeating of an opponent. The ancients called it the "Argument of the Cudgel," because of its resemblance to the most ancient form of argument—that of beating one's opponent with a club, or a resort to fisticuffs, both being favorite forms of argument in some circles. The cave-man, and his modern prototype favors the plan of argument which consists of beating into submission those who differ with them in opinion. Jevons says: "An attorney for the defendant in a lawsuit is said to have handed to the barrister his brief marked, 'No case; abuse the plaintiff's attorney.' Whoever uses an argument which rests, not upon the merit of the case, but the character or position of those engaged in it, commits this fallacy. If a man is accused of a crime it is no answer to say that the prosecutor is bad." It is no argument to say in reply to a charge; that "those who live in glass houses should not throw stones;" or to answer, "you're another!" It is a favorite method of some public speakers to answer a charge, or a proposition, by attacking the character of those advancing it. Some scientific writers have charged their clerical opponents with frequently resorting to this form of false argument, instead of meeting argument with argument. There is no excuse for this practice, by whomever employed.

XI. *Argument by Complex Questions*. This form of false argument consists of asking questions of the opponent, or witness, which are so worded as to entangle him in a paradox, or else to cause him to appear to make damaging statements by the application of the answer of one question to another. Often the question is so cleverly worded that an answer of either "Yes" or "No" places the answerer in a false position. For instance, the well known trick-question of the lawyer who asked the witness the question: "Have you stopped beating your mother?" to which an answer either in the affirmative or negative would have been an admission of a detestable offense. A similar question is: "Then you have turned honest?" or "You have learned to tell the truth at last, have you?" Many questions may be asked in a "double form," so that an answer of either "Yes" or "No" will give a false impression, the only escape being to answer each part of the question separately. Brooks says of this form of false argument: "This is a low trick sometimes employed by lawyers in the examination of witnesses, with a view of puzzling them or turning their answers to a wrong account. Thus, 'You were swayed by the love of money in the transaction?' (meaning exclusively), to which the witness answers, "Yes" (meaning in part). Another question follows: 'In being swayed by money you acted selfishly in the transaction?' The utilitarian puts to us the questions: 'You deny that virtue consists in utility!' 'Yes.' 'Then you deny that utility is a good thing.'" This form of "tripping up" one's opponent is characteristic of those who prefer to win by "smartness" rather than by intellect. A certain form of argumentative questioning, designed to bring out points which may be attacked, is allowable and quite fair and proper—the line between the fair and unfair is very plainly marked, however.

XII. *Argument against the Professions of the Opponent.* This form of false argument consists in appealing from the point at issue, to the professions, principles, or previously expressed opinions of the opponent. For instance, a Freethinker or an Atheist may be defending an orthodox theological doctrine as strictly logical and consistent with correct reasoning from the accepted premises. It is no argument, or answer, against the truth of the proposition, to say "Why, you are an Atheist or Freethinker! You do not believe in the Scriptures upon which you are basing your argument!" In the same way, it is no answer or argument to assert that a defender of a Republican principle happens to be a Democrat. Nor is a drunkard stopped from logically asserting the principles of Temperance or Prohibition. The fallacy in this form of false argument lies in the fact that while the answer *is valid as against the opponent*, and may silence, or confuse him, and create an impression against his reasoning; it *is not valid against the question at issue*, or the views advocated by him—the logic of his argument is not affected in the least degree. It is not an argument *ad rem*, that is, directed toward the real issue, and therefore has no logical value in determining the matter. The proof of the fallacious nature of this form of argument or answer is that *when the opponent changes his views, beliefs, or opinions*, the argument falls to the ground, while the original points at issue are unchanged, showing that there is no logical connection between the two. Brooks says: "This fallacy is especially objectionable when we take advantage of premises which those with whom we argue allow, but which we ourselves do not believe. It is legitimate only when we wish to make our opponents doubt their premises by seeing the consequences to which they lead, or to silence an unreasoning and caviling adversary. * * * Christ often used this method to silence the cavils of the Jews, as in Matt. xxii:41–45."

XIII. *Argument of Assumed Authority.* This form of false reasoning consists in appealing to the feeling or veneration, reverence, respect, or assumed authority entertained by the hearers. For example, the argument that the contention must be true for it is asserted in a certain reverenced book, or other writing; has been asserted by some venerated person, or respected person, such as: "We find it in Shakespeare;" "Plato has asserted its truth;" "Your fathers before you have always believed it;" "The president has expressed himself in favor of its truth;" "The clergy unite in affirming the proposition;" etc. Brooks says: "Thus the scholastics employed the maxim, 'It is foolish to affirm that Aristotle erred;' and in the same manner the conservative argues against any improvement in society or the state by referring to the opinions of the fathers of the republic. The argument may be used to prevent any rash disturbance of the social order; but it is in every case a fallacy." Hyslop says that it "is an appeal to authority, or body of accepted doctrines. It is valid for producing conviction when the authority is accepted by the persons to whom the appeal is addressed, but it is not *ad rem* proof, and when not accepted by anyone is still more glaring * * *" This form of false argument must not be confused with the valid and proper reference *to real authority as evidence*, as for instance the opinion of expert witnesses; legal decisions of learned judges; opinions of eminent medical men; conclusions of eminent scientists; or other views of men learned in their particular lines, concerning their own respective specialties. This last mentioned class of opinions have weight as corroborative evidence or proof, and may properly be considered in forming a judgment. But *the opinion of anyone does not logically prove the truth of a proposition.* At the best *opinion* is far removed from *actual knowledge of facts.*

In addition to the above instances of False Argument, there are others arising from Inductive Reasoning, which being rather technical and concerned rather with Logic than Argumentative Discourse, we shall not consider here. Some of these, however, have been indicated in their appropriate place in preceding chapters. It is thought well, however, to add the following quotations from two eminent authorities:

Concerning the fallacies arising from false analogy, Jevons says: "It is impossible too often to remind people that on the one hand *all correct reasoning consists in substituting like things for like things*, and inferring that what is true of one will be true of all which are similar to it in the points of resemblance concerned in the matter. *All incorrect reasoning, on the other hand, consists in putting one thing for another when there is not the requisite likeness.* It is the purpose of the rules of deductive and inductive logic to enable us to judge as far as possible when we are thus rightly or wrongly reasoning from some things to others."

Hyslop says, regarding Inference: "We cannot infer anything we please from any premises we please. We must conform to certain definite rules or principles. Any violation of them will be a fallacy. * * * There are, then, two simple rules which should not be violated. (1) *The subject-matter in the conclusion should be of the same general kind, as in the premises.* (2) *The facts constituting the premises must be accepted, and must not be fictitious.*"

If we may be pardoned for venturing an additional rule after these of the two eminent authorities just mentioned, we should say: *Beware of too hasty generalization; beware of false generalization.* Because one woman is a coquette, it is not just to accuse all women of a tendency to indulge in flirtation. Because one man has lied to you, it is not just to assert that "all men are liars." Because one Irishman has red hair and blue eyes, it is not right to generalize that all Irishmen have fiery locks and violet eyes. Because you may handle a large blue-bottle fly with impunity, it does not follow that you can do the same with a bumble-bee which is about the same size, flies in a similar manner, and makes about the same kind of noise. Hasty generalization is the sign of an untrained mind—children are particularly addicted to it. And argument based on hasty generalization is often false by reason of its false premises. Argument, like the house in the parable, must be built upon the solid rock of a valid premise, and not on the shifting sand of fictitious and unaccepted premises arising from hasty generalization and inference. If the foundation is false, the structure is false. Be sure that your fundamental facts are right—then "go ahead."

CHAPTER XIV.

Emotional Appeal

THE FIFTH step in Argumentative Discourse is that known as *the Appeal to the Emotions*. To many this may appear to be outside of the true province of the Argument, and in the nature of an unwarranted artifice by means of which the understanding is clouded by the force of feeling. But it must be remembered that the majority of people really employ their reasoning faculties to a comparatively limited degree, and that they are dependent to a considerable extent upon the moving force of their feelings or emotions in forming a judgment or in taking action. It has been said by thoughtful men that the majority of the race employ reason merely as a means of justifying their feelings or excusing their actions, instead of as a means of determining judgment and action. They fail to observe the rule laid down by Caird that: "That which enters the heart must first be discerned by the *intelligence* to be *true*. It must be seen as having in its own nature a *right* to dominate feeling and as constituting the principle by which feeling must be judged."

It has been said that "men do not seek *reasons*—they demand only *excuses* to justify the feelings and actions." Halleck says: "Belief is a mental state which might as well be classed under emotion as under thinking, for it combines both elements. Belief is part inference from the known to the unknown, and part feeling or emotion. Wherever the proof of anything is not absolute, but where the probability seems to our minds to be of the strongest kind, we are said to *believe*. We can absolutely prove much that has occurred in the past. It is not a matter of belief, but of absolute knowledge, that a certain building was burned, that a certain man died, that it rained yesterday, that there was ice last winter. When we come to consider the future, we are thrown more or less on a state of belief. From the thought processes involved in comparing and inferring, we find ourselves *feeling* more or less sure that certain things will happen in the future. Ask a farmer who is sowing a certain crop if he is absolutely sure that sufficient rain will fall for the crop, and he will reply that he is not sure, but that he believes that there will be rain. * * * So long as the world does not stagnate, it will always act on belief in the most weighty matters, whether of religion or of business."

The same authority also says regarding the effect of emotion upon intellectual action: "On the one hand, the emotions are favorable to intellectual action, since they supply the interest one feels in study. One may feel intensely concerning a certain subject and be all the better student. Hence the emotions are not, as was formerly thought, entirely hostile to intellectual action. Emotion often quickens the perception, burns things indelibly into the memory, and doubles the rapidity of thought. On the other hand, strong feelings often vitiate every operation of the intellect. They cause us to see only what we wish to, to remember only what we wish to, to remember only what interests our narrow feelings at the time, and to reason from selfish data only * * * Emotion puts the magnifying end of the telescope to our intellectual eye where our own interests are concerned, the minimizing end when we are looking at the interests of others."

What is true of the individual regarding the effect and power of feeling and emotion, is doubly true of the crowd. Those who have studied the subject of "the psychology of the crowd" know that when people are gathered together in a crowd or assemblage they are peculiarly liable to emotional excitement, and "emotional contagion." As Prof. Davenport says: "The mind of the crowd is strangely like that of primitive man. Most of the people in it may be far from primitive in emotion, in thought, in character; nevertheless, the result always tends to be the same. Stimulation immediately begets action. Reason is in abeyance. The cool, rational speaker has little chance beside the skillful, emotional orator. The crowd thinks in images, and speech must take this form to be accessible to it. The images are not connected by any natural bond, and they take each other's place like the slides of a magic lantern. It follows from this, of course, that appeals to the imagination have paramount influence. The crowd is united and governed by emotion rather than by reason. Emotion is the natural bond, for men differ much less in this respect than in intellect. It is also true that in a crowd of a thousand men the amount of emotion actually generated and existing is far greater than the sum which might conceivably be obtained by adding together the emotion of the individuals taken by themselves. * * * As in the case of the primitive mind, imagination has unlocked the floodgates of emotion, which on occasion may become wild enthusiasm or demoniac frenzy."

Recognizing the psychological effect of appeals to the emotion and feelings, the best authorities are of the opinion that it would be folly to leave this effective weapon in the hands of unscrupulous demagogues, and to unworthy causes. They feel that the weapon should be employed for good and worthy purposes as well as for those of the opposite character. And so we find that the best speakers employ this phase of discoursive expression, often with great effect.

Burke says: "In painting, we may represent any fine figure we please; but we never can give it those enlivening touches which we may receive from words. To represent an angel in a picture, you can only draw a beautiful young man winged, but what painting can furnish us any thing so grand as the addition of one word, 'the angel of the *Lord?*' * * * Now as there is a moving tone of voice, an impassioned countenance, an agitated gesture, which affect independently of the things about which they are exerted, so there are words, and certain dispositions of words, which being peculiarly devoted to passionate subjects, and always used by those who are under the influence of any passion, touch and move us more than those which far more clearly and distinctly express the subject matter. We yield to sympathy what we refuse to description."

Halleck gives the following excellent description of the ideas best fitted to raise emotion in the minds of one's hearers: "Feeling cannot be compelled. Even if a person wishes to feel sorry, he cannot merely because some one tells him he should. There must be an adequate cause, just as so much fuel must be consumed to raise the temperature of water a given number of degrees. Many would-be orators rave and gesticulate wildly, but excite no emotion save disgust in their hearers. * * * A large part of the business of life consists in moving the emotions of men so as to get them to act. Those ideas which give vivid pictures of a concrete act of injustice, of the doer of a noble deed, of an actual sufferer, seldom fail to raise emotion. If a man intends to get a contribution for the sick poor, let him not speak in general terms of the inconvenience of sickness, the pains of poverty. One vivid picture of a forlorn room where a feeble mother is watching her sick child, for whom she is unable to procure proper food, will be infinitely more effective. Any idea which suggests gratification of desire, any idea which vividly pictures something affecting the welfare of the self or of others, is apt to be followed by emotion. Probably no one can even imagine a person in a burning car, or lying helpless with broken limbs on a lonely road, without feeing the emotion of pity arise."

Whitefield, the eminent preacher, possessed this art of painting emotional word pictures to a wonderful degree. This, coupled with his dramatic instinct, was probably the secret of his great power over people. An English writer once said of him: "Wherein lies the secret of Whitefield's power? What was the spell by which he not only enthralled the multitude, but also men of clear judgments and capacious intellects and cold hearts? When we read Whitefield's sermons we find nothing in them that explains this mystery. He was not a theologian; he was not a thinker; he had no high poetical imagination; his diction is commonplace; his imagery conventional; his range of illustration limited; and it is remarkable that he has left nothing in literature, not even in devotional literature, by which he deserves to be remembered—not a single treatise, not a hymn, not a page of discourse. Face to face with men he did with them as he chose, but he had no skill to sway them by written words."

The following, from the pen of Nathan Sheppard, will give you the answer regarding the nature and source of Whitefield's power:

"Whitefield came nearer to the Demosthenic standard than is possible with many speakers of our western race. He utilized the histrionic art in public speaking beyond any other preacher of his age and tongue. The actors heard him with envy. Garrick was jealous of the skill and grace with which he handled his handkerchief. His manners, it is said, captivated the fastidious Chesterfield, he extorted admiration from the philosophical Bolingbroke, and the elegant skeptic, David Hume, went great distances to hear doctrines that he detested delivered in a style that fascinated him.

"When Whitefield acted an old blind man advancing by slow steps toward the edge of the precipice, Lord Chesterfield started up and cried: 'Good God, he is gone!' And when the seaman heard and saw his description of the ship on her beam-ends, they sprang to their feet and shouted: 'The long-boat—take to the long-boat!' This scene is worth reproducing. Suddenly assuming a nautical air and manner that were irresistible, he broke in with: 'Well, my boys, we have a clear sky, and are making fine headway over a smooth sea before a light breeze, and we shall soon lose sight of land. But what means this—this sudden lowering of the heavens, and that dark cloud arising from beneath the western horizon? Hark! Don't you hear distant thunder! Don't you see those flashes of lightning! There is a storm gathering! Every man to his duty! How the waves rise and dash against the ship! The air is dark!—the tempest rages!— our masts are gone!—the ship is on her beam-ends! What next!' This appeal instantly brought the sailors to their feet, with a shout: 'The long-boat—take to the long-boat!'"

Benjamin Franklin, in his "Autobiography," tells the following story of Whitefield's power over the emotions of men: "Returning northward, he preached up this charity and made large collections, for his eloquence had a wonderful power over the hearts and purses of his hearers, of which I, myself, was an instance. I did not approve of the design. * * * but he was resolute in his first project, rejected my counsel, and I refused to contribute. I happened soon after to attend one of his sermons in the course of which I perceived he intended to finish with a collection, and I silently resolved he should get nothing from me. I had in my pocket a handful of copper money, three or four silver dollars, and five pistoles in gold. As he proceeded I began to soften and concluded to give the coppers. Another stroke of his oratory made me ashamed of that and determined me to give the silver; and he finished so admirably that I emptied my pockets wholly into the collector's dish, gold and all."

Mr. Sheppard gives the following suggestion regarding the cultivation of the dramatic element in public speaking: "It can be cultivated by the cultivation of the elocutionary instinct, the rhetorical instinct, the dramatic instinct, by the training of the ear for rhetoric and the eye for rhetorical and dramatic effects.

Imitation helps, and observation plays its part, but if the art of the actors and the art of the speakers are confounded, and you undertake to acquire one by acquiring the other, you will acquire neither. * * * To repeat, so as to prevent misconception or confusion: First, the self-excitation or physical earnestness of the actor is just as desirable and valuable to the speaker as it is to the actor; second, the dramatic manner, which is inseparable from the drama, is a very useful auxiliary to public speaking; but, third, when and by whom this dramatic manner is to be used is to be left to the judgment of the speaker; and fourth, that judgment may be trained to an indefinite extent."

And, so say we:

In conclusion, let us consider the words of Cardinal Newman, who said: "Deductions have no power of persuasion. The heart is commonly reached, not through the reason, but through the imagination, by means of direct impressions, by the testimony of facts and events, by history, by description. Persons influence us, voices melt us, looks subdue us, deeds inflame us."

CHAPTER XV.

THE CLOSING TALE

THE SIXTH step in Argumentative Discourse is that known as the *Peroration or Closing,* in which the speaker sums up all that has been said, and strives to forcibly impress upon the mind of his hearers a clear, strong idea of his side of the case—the spirit and essence of his argument; in fact, as Hyslop well says: "Just as definition introduces discourse, recapitulation should close it * * * a recapitulation which sums up in outline all the arguments which have been presented." To many speakers, the opening and the closing steps are the most difficult. As Hill says: "It is in Exordiums and Perorations that a young writer (or speaker) often fails; *he does not know* how to get at his subject or how to get away from it. He should beware of putting in a word of introduction that is not necessary to prepare the way for his argument, and of adding a word at the end that is not necessary to enforce his conclusion. 'Is he never going to begin?' 'Will he never have done?' are questions equally fatal."

In the recapitulation, the subject of the entire argument should be gone over, clearly and briefly, bringing out each important and telling point with emphasis, and passing over the minor points with but a brief mention. Beware of repeating the argument in closing—the time for details of argument has passed. Instead, treat the argument as closed, and assume the tone and manner of one reciting the "accomplished fact" of proof of the various points in dispute. The closing should be a summing up of successful argument—the recapitulation of points scored. It should ever be pitched to the triumphal key— the note of success should be heard throughout it.

In the closing talk, as in the sentence or paragraph, the speaker should seek to emphasize the main points and ideas, and subordinate the less important ones. And just as his paragraphs should be arranged with the idea of moving from the less important and less interesting points to the more important and more interesting, so in his closing he should move forward from the less interesting and less important toward those of a greater degree of importance and interest, until at last the climax is reached, and the discourse ends. That is, it *should* end there—but alas! too many are "unable to let go," and after the climax is reached they persist in continuing, thus bringing about an anti-climax and weakening what would otherwise have been an effective closing. Follow this rule: *When you have said all that is of importance, and have reached your climax—stop! Every word uttered after this point is reached, weakens what you have already said.*

The study of the closing parts of the speeches of well-known orators will be valuable to the student in pointing out by actual example the technique of the peroration or closing talk. Far more may be thus gained from actual example than from stated rules or formal methods. The spirit of effective oratory is contagious—one's torch must be lighted at that of a predecessor.

It is customary to close the discourse with an earnest appeal which brings the climax to a head. This is the closing chord— the final note of the trumpet. It should, if possible, be prepared and fixed in the mind before the argument is commenced. Just as the opening talk should be prepared after the discourse itself is fully mapped, so it is well to prepare the peroration or closing paragraph before the final mapping out of the argument. It should be the goal toward which the argument travels. It should be the crown which is sought for in the struggle of the discourse.

The following passage was used by Lord Brougham in closing his speech defending Queen Caroline, and was the result of previous study and preparation on his part—some authorities stating that it was rewritten over twenty times before its delivery:

"Such, my lords, is the case now before you! Such is the evidence in support of this measure—evidence inadequate to prove a debt—impotent to deprive of a civil right—ridiculous to convict of the lowest offence—scandalous if brought forward to support a charge of the highest nature which the law knows—monstrous to ruin the honor, to blast the name of an English Queen! What shall I say, then, if this is the proof by which an act of judicial legislation, a parliamentary sentence, an *ex post facto* law, is sought to be passed against this defenceless woman? My lords, I pray you to pause. I do earnestly beseech you to take heed! You are standing on the brink of a precipice—then beware! It will go forth your judgment, if sentence shall go against the queen. But It will be the only judgment you ever pronounced, which, instead of reaching its object, will return and bound back upon those who give it. Save the country, my lords, from the horrors of this catastrophe—save yourselves from this peril—rescue that country, of which you are the ornaments, but in which you can flourish no longer, when severed from the people, than the blossom when cut off from the roots and the stem of the tree. Save that country, that you may continue to adorn it—save the Crown, which is in jeopardy—the Aristocracy, which is shaken—save the Altar, which must stagger with the blow that rends its kindred Throne! You have said, my lords, you have willed—the Church and the King have willed—that the Queen shall be deprived of its solemn service. She has instead of that solemnity, the heartfelt prayers of the people. She wants no prayers of mine. But I do here pour forth my humble supplication at the Throne of Mercy, that that Mercy may be poured down upon the people, in a larger measure than the merits of their rulers may deserve, and that your hearts may be turned to justice!"